NEW DIRECTIONS FOR COMMUNITY COLLEGES

Arthur M. Cohen
EDITOR-IN-CHIEF

Florence B. Brawer
ASSOCIATE EDITOR

Prisoners of Elitism: The Community College's Struggle for Stature

Billie Wright Dziech
University of Cincinnati

William R. Vilter
University of Cincinnati

EDITORS

Number 78, Summer 1992

JOSSEY-BASS PUBLISHERS
San Francisco

EDUCATIONAL RESOURCES INFORMATION CENTER

Clearinghouse For Junior Colleges

UNIVERSITY OF CALIFORNIA, LOS ANGELES

PRISONERS OF ELITISM: THE COMMUNITY COLLEGE'S STRUGGLE FOR STATURE
Billie Wright Dziech, William R. Vilter (eds.)
New Directions for Community Colleges, no. 78
Volume XX, number 2
Arthur M. Cohen, Editor-in-Chief
Florence B. Brawer, Associate Editor

Microfilm copies of issues and articles are available in 16mm and 35mm, as well as microfiche in 105mm, through University Microfilms Inc., 300 North Zeeb Road, Ann Arbor, Michigan 48106.

LC 85-644753   ISSN 0194-3081   ISBN 1-55542-750-2

NEW DIRECTIONS FOR COMMUNITY COLLEGES is part of The Jossey-Bass Higher and Adult Education Series and is published quarterly by Jossey-Bass Inc., Publishers, 350 Sansome Street, San Francisco, California 94104-1310 (publication number USPS 121-710) in association with the ERIC Clearinghouse for Junior Colleges. Second-class postage paid at San Francisco, California, and at additional mailing offices. POSTMASTER: Send address changes to New Directions for Community Colleges, Jossey-Bass Inc., Publishers, 350 Sansome Street, San Francisco, California 94104-1310.

SUBSCRIPTIONS for 1992 cost $48.00 for individuals and $70.00 for institutions, agencies, and libraries.

THE MATERIAL in this publication is based on work sponsored wholly or in part by the Office of Educational Research and Improvement, U.S. Department of Education, under contract number RI-88-062002. Its contents do not necessarily reflect the views of the Department, or any other agency of the U.S. Government.

EDITORIAL CORRESPONDENCE should be sent to the Editor-in-Chief, Arthur M. Cohen, at the ERIC Clearinghouse for Junior Colleges, University of California, Los Angeles, California 90024.

Cover photograph by Rene Sheret, Los Angeles, California © 1990.

The paper used in this journal is acid-free and meets the strictest guidelines in the United States for recycled paper (50 percent recycled waste, including 10 percent post-consumer waste). Manufactured in the United States of America.

045718

Contents

Editors' Notes

When one spends a quarter of a century working in a two-year college that is part of one of the nation's largest universities, concerns about status inevitably arise. At the University of Cincinnati's University College, the struggle for recognition and respect can be a daily fact of life; and, occasionally, on bad days, it has occurred to both of us that we are, in a very real sense, prisoners of elitism. At those times, whether we, in University College, are better or worse off than our colleagues in community colleges geographically distant from the benefits of a large university seems less important to us than whether or not our colleagues across campus understand our mission and value our contributions to scholarship and teaching.

Some of these university colleagues assume that the community college movement burst without precedent upon the higher education scene in 1960, when University College was founded. Others know better, since higher education scholars have exhibited increasing interest in tracing the historical development of the community college. Assuming that the search for roots might produce understanding of contemporary problems and insight into strategic planning for the future, these scholars have examined the contribution of Thomas Jefferson, the evolution of land grant colleges under the 1862 and 1980 Morrill Acts, the impact of the post–World War II G.I. Bill of Rights, the 1947 report of the Truman Commission on Higher Education for American Democracy, the 1958 National Defense Education Act, and the 1965 and 1968 Higher Education Acts and later amendments. Each, in its own unique way, contributed to the community college as we currently know it.

But what is evident in most of these historical surveys is that American colleges and universities were of an elitist bent long before the opening of the first junior college. Walter Crosby Eells, an early historian of the community college movement, provided the following scenario. As early as 1852, Henry P. Tappan, president of the University of Michigan, suggested the need to differentiate between upper-division and lower-division collegiate work. In his mind, the upper division was vastly superior to the lower. Tappan's call for differentiation was followed in 1869 by that of W. W. Folwell, president of the University of Minnesota. In 1882, William Rainey Harper, president of the University of Chicago, opened his Academic College for Freshmen and Sophomores, which became known in 1886 as the Junior College. Very soon after, the University of Chicago founded two-year affiliates in Joliet, Illinois, and in Goshen, Indiana, and Harper became known as "the father" of the two-year college movement (Eells, 1931, pp. 45–47).

When these three nineteenth-century university presidents examined their institutions, they saw what seemed to be serious problems associated with managing their universities' curricula. As a response, they suggested a move toward the "bifurcated university," to use Medsker's (1960, p. 11) expression, because they preferred to get on with the business of educating the elite. What was taking place in the Midwest was not lost on the academic "reformers" on the East and West coasts. As reported by Eells (1931, pp. 48–49), the president of Stanford said in 1904 that "the [lower-division] College is part of the dividing trunk of which the University represents the fruiting branches." The elitist orientation of F. J. Goodnow, president of Johns Hopkins University, was apparent in his Commemoration Day address of 1925: "The instruction in the first two years has probably always been in essence what is known as secondary rather than advanced instruction. In that account it has no proper place in a university as distinguished from a college. Under present conditions where this kind of instruction is given to masses of somewhat immature minds in probably the largest school of the modern American university, the development of the best kind of advanced work is made difficult if not impossible" (Eells, 1931, p. 51).

In typically American fashion, opponents of this elitism began to make themselves heard. Alexis F. Lange, dean of the Department of Education at the University of California at Berkeley and a leader in the development of California's junior college system, clearly disagreed with his colleagues about the virtue of lower-division instruction and of junior colleges: "One thing is clear. No university department must be allowed to direct or prescribe for the corresponding junior-college department. My own strong conviction is that the junior college can, and should, be something better than a conglomerate of departments pursuing a hodgepodge of aims. To forestall such a development, the university will have to do more adjusting in its lower division than the junior college should be expected to do" (Lange, [1916] 1950, p. 349).

By 1924, academic research was being generated to counter apparent elitist concern about the need to ensure that high standards were applied to two-year college graduates. In that year, using what seems even today to be a scrupulous research design, L. V. Koos (1924, p. 237) reported that "there seems to be no appreciable difference in the degrees of success in the work of their junior years of junior college graduates and of those who do their first two years work in a standard university."

Koos also noted in 1925 that the supporters of the junior college were beginning to devalue the elitist model and to establish new academic and social functions for the college. As he said, many of these supporters "expect more of it than that it shall be a mere neck of land between two larger bodies of land" (Koos, 1925, p. 16). Koos admitted that in the bulletins of the colleges this "isthmian function" was still dominant. At the same time, he also identified in the college bulletins and in the periodical literature of the day several emerging functions. Among these were the rounding out of general education, vocational training, the popularization of higher education, the development of maturity in a home environment, individualized education, and better instruction.

Nineteen years later, Koos was still at work countering potential elitist detractors of the community college movement. In 1944, discussing what he termed the junior college's "democratization of education," Koos reported on twelve thousand high school graduates from sixty-one high schools in twelve states. The results of the study clearly demonstrated the value to society of the two-year college. He found that in school systems with nearby junior colleges the percentage of graduates entering college was 2.5 times greater than for systems without junior colleges. For the upper socioeconomic group, the rate of attendance was 1.5 times larger; for the lower socioeconomic group, the rate was 3.5 times larger (Koos, 1944, pp. 273–276). These data indicated that the "opportunity colleges" were giving members of America's lower socioeconomic classes a chance to express their desire for social mobility (Medsker, 1960, p. 18). George Keller (1983, p. 9) reinforced this contention when he asserted,

> [In the twenty years between 1955 and 1974], by building a new two-year college every two weeks, America created a new form of college-going for nearly 40 percent of those in higher education—a form still unique to the United States. The new community college sector shielded the older four-year colleges and universities from many of the rising pressures of vocationalism and job training, from admissions for the less academically qualified, from vast increases in financial aid for the sons and daughters of the poor and minorities, and from much of the new pattern of part-time higher education and adult education.

Given the tension that has so long characterized relations between two- and four-year institutions, it is both ironic and significant that the University of Chicago, one of the most prestigious of the nation's baccalaureate and graduate degree-granting institutions, was the original home to the two-year college movement. The irony is that so many baccalaureate institutions, from the least to the most renowned, have at times regarded community colleges with arrogance and suspicion. The significance is that at the turn of another century, almost one hundred years later, community colleges and institutions like the University of Chicago are increasingly forced to recognize that their individual survival, as well as that of the American way of life, depends on resolution of differences, interdependence, and a moratorium on the academic elitism in which institutions, students, and faculty have been imprisoned for far too long.

"Forced recognition" is a significant expression here, for it would be foolhardy to imply that the typical engineering or classics professor at a major research or Ivy League institution has been struck by a vision of egalitarianism so compelling that he or she honestly believes that the pro- totypical two-year college student belongs in higher education. On the other hand, community college faculty serving in the depths of rural or inner-city America probably also harbor doubts about their students and about their own abilities to transform their charges into the educated, skilled workers mandated by a changing economy. But necessity is the mother of invention; and if ever there was a time in our history when we were called upon by necessity to become inventive, it is now.

By the year 2000, in less than a decade, the demographics and the workplace of America will have altered so radically that effective education may be, in most respects, our society's only hope to accommodate all of the changes and survive intact. If education is to work, however, the old elitist notions, the unjustified distinctions drawn between two-year and four-year institutions and educators, will no longer suffice. This claim is not to imply that differences among students will cease but rather that higher education will be called upon as never before to engage in inven- tion, which the dictionary defines as "the act of finding out, discovery . . . the power to conceive and present new combinations of facts or ideas."

Discovery begins with introspection, and when we of the community college examine ourselves with objectivity, we must begin by acknowledging that our modest position in the higher education hierarchy is due, at least in part, to our own choices and behaviors. We rail against baccalaureate colleagues for not comprehending our faculty's exhaustion and exaspera- tion at being required to carry twelve- to fifteen-hour teaching loads. We boast about our commitment to students and our dedication to teaching. Yet many of us are less loquacious when someone introduces the topics of research and publication; we are willing to listen to K. Patricia Cross advo- cate classroom research, but actually doing it is a less convenient matter. And so our excellence goes unshared, undocumented.

We may resist the analogy to business, but we in two-year institutions have not marketed ourselves very well to our baccalaureate colleagues. Our achievements generally surpass our failures, but we have been too enam- ored of the old baccalaureate ways of conducting business. Perhaps we, as they, have forgotten Will Rogers's admonition: "Even if you're on the right track, you'll get run over if you just sit there." Too many of us have "just sat" too long, either blind to the power of innovation and creativity or immune to the realities of our successes. Often we have acquiesced to the unwar- ranted assumption that community and junior colleges are "second best." In so doing, we have allowed not only ourselves but also our students and their educations to be regarded as mediocre.

The contributions to this volume, *Prisoners of Elitism: The Community College's Struggle for Stature,* are exciting because they are written by indi- viduals who have refused to accept the myth of second best. These are men and women who have been involved with the community and junior college movement in a variety of ways and have sought new combinations of ideas, better ways of educating and serving increasingly heterogeneous constituencies in an ever more complex world. Recurrent throughout their chapters is an understanding of the revolution that higher education is undergoing and a conviction that two-year colleges possess the expertise and the experience to exert leadership in the days ahead.

Gustavo A. Mellander and Bruce Robertson, in Chapter One, concentrate on teaching, the most crucial mission of the community college. They trace the historical development of its approach to instruction and describe the tensions that occurred between two- and four-year institutions as the former carved out pedagogical identities suited to the talents and needs of their diverse constituencies. The authors conclude by offering examples of creative, farsighted programs that attest the superior ability of community colleges to transform the teaching function and reach new consumers of higher education.

George B. Vaughan, in Chapter Two, deals with an area in which the community college has been less successful in achieving stature. Acknowledging that only a minority of two-year faculty and administrators engage in research and publication, he maintains that the real need in academia is for community college, as well as four-year, higher education professionals to promote and to involve themselves in "scholarship." He explains why scholarship has not been perceived as intrinsic to two-year college culture and offers recommendations for making it a more "integral ingredient in community college philosophy."

One area in which two-year institutions have had too little power is articulation agreements. In Chapter Three, Roger J. Barry and Phyllis A. Barry acknowledge that, in transfer decision making, community colleges have truly been prisoners of the elitist notions of baccalaureate institutions. They provide examples of successful transfer programs and argue that if two-year colleges are to escape the bonds imposed by four-year educators, they "must lobby for and demand strong state-mandated articulation agreements so they can negotiate on an equal basis with universities."

Carolyn Prager, in Chapter Four, decries critics who blame low transfer rates on the environment, policies, and students of the community college and asserts that accreditation bodies must share some of the blame for the "transfer malaise." She maintains that they can act as agents for change by strongly encouraging or mandating that senior institutions facilitate articulation, that occupational faculty in two-year colleges be educated beyond the associate and possibly the baccalaureate degree level, and that career curricula include sound general education components. Only then, Prager claims, will four-year institutions face the responsibility for reducing transfer barriers and two-year institutions be freed of the burden of having to "go it alone."

Gwen May and Al Smith, in Chapter Five, demonstrate that relations

between two- and four-year institutions are not inevitably marked by difficulty. After outlining the history of interinstitutional cooperation and com-
menting on the benefits it can bring to community colleges, they examine
five consortia that have succeeded in increasing the stature and effectiveness of community colleges. May and Smith close by asserting that "the
strength, the stature, and the potential of [two- and four-year] institutions
lie in working together."

In Chapter Six, James O. Hammons argues that community colleges
have concentrated too much energy on impressing baccalaureate institutions. Genuine stature, he contends, can be achieved only when two-year
institutions define excellence for themselves and focus on "impressing
themselves and their communities with their worth." He then outlines
twelve qualities that constitute excellence, which he defines as "accomplishing one's mission, goals, and objectives in a cost-efficient manner,
while maintaining a positive institutional climate for staff and students."

Diane Hirshberg, in Chapter Seven, concludes by providing an overview of current materials in the ERIC data base on the topics of community
college-university collaboration and on issues of excellence in the community college.

Each of the authors reminds us that the community college is not
about to be defeated by the forces of elitism, and that it is equally
undaunted by the grave educational problems confronting us. The chapters
demonstrate that the struggle for stature begins on an individual level and
that, with courage and commitment, we of the community college can
make a difference—in our baccalaureate colleagues' perceptions of our
work and in the educations of those who have trusted us to prepare them
for the challenges of tomorrow.

Billie Wright Dziech
William R. Vilter
Editors

References

Eells, W. C. *The Junior College.* New York: Houghton Mifflin, 1931.

Keller, G. *Academic Strategy: The Management Revolution in American Higher Education.* Balti-
more, Md.: Johns Hopkins University Press, 1983. (ED 236 977)

Koos, L. V. *The Junior College.* Minneapolis: University of Minnesota Press, 1924.

Koos, L. V. *The Junior College Movement.* Boston: Ginn, 1925.

Koos, L. V. "How to Democratize the Junior College Level." *School Review,* 1944, *50* (5), 271–
284.

Lange, A. F. "The Junior College, with Special Reference to California." In J. P. Bogue (ed.),
The Community College. New York: McGraw-Hill, 1950. (Originally published 1916).

Medsker, L. L. *The Junior College: Progress and Prospect.* New York: McGraw-Hill, 1960.

BILLIE WRIGHT DZIECH is assistant to the dean and professor of English at the University of Cincinnati's University College.

WILLIAM R. VILTER is head of the Department of Language Arts and associate professor of English at the University of Cincinnati's University College.

New legislative and social realities will move community college faculty to assert their unique commitment to teaching and compel their baccalaureate colleagues to respect their efforts.

Tradition and Transformation: Academic Roots and the Community College Future

Gustavo A. Mellander, Bruce Robertson

When community colleges were originally developed, they had their roots in our democratic public school system but their aspirations in the more elitist world of four-year colleges and universities. From the beginning, their faculty faced the problem of how to define their roles and responsibilities. They could emulate the traditions of the four-year institutions to which their students would transfer; they could operate within the framework of elementary and secondary education, under whose jurisdiction their governance was first placed; or they could develop their own style and traditions.

Community college faculty also had a unique opportunity. They could combine the best of the two worlds of high school and college teaching. Primarily, they were going to be teachers, but teachers who could use the collegiate portion of their tradition to break away from the constraints and petty regulations of secondary school teaching and yet, at the same time, avoid the pitfall of the research university with its pious faith that faculty selected according to their abilities as researchers are automatically effective teachers.

Community college faculty were, in a sense, compelled to emphasize teaching because their educational mission was so complex. Unlike the baccalaureate institutions, the community colleges offered occupational programs, usually built around local rather than national labor markets. These required different faculty and different teaching practices from those found in typical undergraduate colleges. The community colleges, and

NEW DIRECTIONS FOR COMMUNITY COLLEGES, no. 78, Summer 1992 ©Jossey-Bass Publishers their faculty, grew increasingly responsive to the needs and interests of adult learners, who required different teaching techniques and more flexible scheduling. In addition, they rapidly added remedial and noncollegiate courses and became the second-chance institutions for students either denied access to or unable to succeed at the four-year institutions. In the process, the community college faculty experimented with and perfected innovative teaching techniques.

Community Colleges: America's Multipurpose Educational Institutions

The changes described above made community colleges quite different from the institutions immediately preceding and following them in the educational hierarchy. High schools were intended for full-time students, continuously enrolled until they received diplomas. High school teachers were full-time teachers who functioned purely as teachers. Four-year colleges were designed for selected high school graduates who enrolled in college immediately upon graduation and subsequently received baccalaureate degrees or else failed or dropped out. College professors, especially after World War II, had a complex array of responsibilities involving research, teaching, institutional governance, and obligations to their academic discipline.

Admittedly, reality was a little less neat than the scenario depicted here. High schools operated adult schools where a few general interest and some remedial courses, leading to a general equivalency diploma or an adult school diploma, were taught. Undergraduate colleges admitted the occasional older student, especially after World War II, and tacitly accepted the fact that quite a few students dropped out for a while or changed colleges before they ultimately got their degrees. But, except for adult schools and a few urban four-year colleges with large evening programs, overwhelmingly both high school and baccalaureate programs were designed for a circumscribed age group of full-time students.

Community colleges, however, evolved into the general purpose institutions of American education. Teaching tended to be an amalgam of collegiate and secondary school practices. The two traditions coexisted uneasily on campus, with tension between the elitist values of the university and the more democratic values of the public schools. On the one hand, community colleges were postsecondary institutions. They offered degrees, they did not compel students to attend, and they established rigorous academic standards. On the other hand, they provided open access and universal collegiate education to the masses. Thus, community colleges stood midway between secondary and baccalaureate education. Open enrollment fulfilled the democratic aspiration of making college available to all, yet only the self-chosen attended, and they had to meet the faculty's academic standards.

For community college faculty, the sorting out of this assemblage of teaching responsibilities was a major task. They needed to distinguish between transfer activities, which were a part of the collegiate world, and nontransfer activities, which were postsecondary by design and developmental or career-oriented in intent. To accomplish this task, they developed new teaching methods and organizational patterns that let them cope with this diversity of programs and levels and yet interfaced effectively with colleges and universities, high schools, the local employment market, and community interests.

Overall, however, the result was confusing. Community colleges had to determine which values and practices should be uppermost: those of baccalaureate institutions, high schools, or the relatively few community colleges that developed new traditions of their own. The tension was continuous, although ultimately community colleges gave greater emphasis to collegiate values. First, they adopted the academic calendar. Although a necessity for transfer programs, it was less suitable for many occupational programs or for meeting the needs of adult learners, who could not afford the more leisurely pace of the academic world.

Second, they adopted the collegiate credit system, which was a mixed blessing. Again, although a necessity for transfer programs, it was inappropriate for many occupational programs. It did not fit occupational programs in which students needed extensive experience. Such programs were forced to labor under the artificial collegiate credit categories such as "laboratory." Thus, long hours of clinical or skill development activities generated heavy faculty workloads and large numbers of student credit hours. Both factors put pressure on programs to curtail vitally needed experiential portions. Another disadvantage was that many occupational courses did not need a three-credit college course time frame and unnecessary "padding" often resulted. A final problem was that some occupational courses, better taught in concentrated time frames, were difficult or impossible to arrange within the traditional academic calendar and credit system.

Third, community colleges incorporated general education requirements into associate degree programs, and some benefits accrued. The addition increased the status of many occupational fields by combining occupational and liberal arts courses into a degree program. It also facilitated transfer. However, it also touched off a perennial conflict about the acceptability of two-year college general education requirements to baccalaureate institutions. There were other disadvantages as well. Two-track occupational certificate programs had to be developed for students who did not want arts and sciences courses. These often emphasized degrees and disregarded the concerns of students who were only interested in individual courses or a portion of a program. While faculty and administrators understood that students could fulfill their educational goals without completing degree or certificate requirements, many legislators and regulatory agencies did not. They reached the incorrect conclusion that occupational programs with large enrollments but few degree recipients were failures.

Fourth, elements of the faculty governance system of the four-year colleges were adopted, and in some institutions these governance practices became virtually indistinguishable from four-year college traditions. Faculty controlled content, textbooks, and grading standards. Within the minimum standards set by transferability requirements, they freely shaped courses to their talents and their students' needs. This autonomy enhanced faculty prestige in the eyes of the students and the community. (It is noteworthy that community colleges and universities, with all their dissimilarities and, generally, without any external academic control except for the peer-reviewed general accreditation process, probably have achieved greater uniformity of standards than has the public school system with its elaborate apparatus of rules and regulations.)

There was one crucial area in which community colleges consciously rejected the practices of baccalaureate institutions: They emphasized teaching over research. The results were that faculty were selected, retained, and promoted on the basis of successful teaching, which became the most essential requirement for advancement, and that course content was less distorted by research interests of faculty or by transitory scholarly trends. Literature courses, for example, reflected the interests of educated readers instead of the internecine warfare between new critics, semioticians, deconstructionists, and several varieties of Marxists. Courses were thus tailored to community interests rather than those of professors; they addressed the interests of heterogeneous populations usually ignored by four-year colleges.

This developing identity of the community college frequently met with disapproval on the four-year college campus. Some baccalaureate faculty, recognizing the differences between themselves and their community college counterparts, defined those counterparts as inferiors. Some recognized differences between their traditional students and transfer students. Transfer students often had different learning styles, modes of expression, and values that were in sharp contrast to those held by traditional students. As four-year college faculty encountered these unfamiliar consumers of education, many tended to associate differences with inferiority. This erroneous association posed no immediate problems for the four-year faculty, however. Elitism can flourish in institutions with supply-demand curves like those that the baccalaureate institutions once had. But now, those curves have flattened, and four-year faculty are compelled to acknowledge that, in many cases, more than half of their graduating seniors began their college work in community colleges. The situation is analogous to the breakup of a monopoly. When the dissolution occurs, competition forces the former employees of the monopoly to learn to work.

New Challenges for American Education

New social trends pose new problems for both community and baccalaureate institutions. Now, too elitist an emphasis will leave community and four-year colleges inappropriately positioned to deal with an educational landscape that is being transformed by several factors. First, the domestic economy of the United States, shifting rapidly as the country adapts to a world economy, has altered the mix of the work force. The number of industrial jobs has declined, the number and variety of service jobs has increased, and the rate of change is rapid. All areas of education are hard-pressed to phase out old programs and introduce new programs that reflect new times. The increased pace of change has put great pressure on faculty and the tenure system. Highly trained and specialized tenured college faculty are not readily able to adjust to rapid change in academic programs; thus, baccalaureate institutions must be prepared to work with their two-year colleagues to meet this new challenge. Second, new immigration has altered the ethnic composition of the American work force and greatly increased the number of young persons and adults for whom English is a second language. In today's international economy, much unskilled labor is performed abroad. This increases the need for a skilled labor force at home. Higher education must reach a multilingual work force, and four-year colleges must accept that two-year institutions possess greater experience and expertise in educating nontraditional students. Third, the educational performance of elementary and secondary school students has declined. If not reversed, this trend will leave the United States with an undereducated population whose skills are not compatible with the needs of the labor market and whose general level of information and literacy may not be appropriate for a democratic society. Remedial teaching, always a component of community college education, must be greatly expanded; and baccalaureate institutions must accept the inevitability of the developmental mission and work with two-year institutions to acknowledge its value.

Impact of Declining Performance in Elementary and Secondary Education on Higher Education

Perhaps the most important problem that higher education faces is the continuing poor performance of students in America's elementary and secondary school systems. The measurable achievement of elementary and secondary students is worse now in virtually every respect than it was twenty years ago, and the achievement of American students is markedly inferior to their counterparts in other Western countries. The decline is not simply a consequence of the flow of new ethnic and social groups into the educational system. It is as common in affluent suburban schools as it is in less wealthy urban schools and is as true of the top 10 percent of the students as it is of the middle and bottom 10 percent.

Reasons for the decline are not difficult to find. The public school system has been inundated with a host of problems, some within the schools, some outside. The overwhelming problems of the schools are new immigration, the task of ending centuries of racial injustice, changes in the structure of the family, the increasing complexity and sophistication of the economy and labor market, unanticipated and undesirable consequences of some of the educational "reforms" of the 1960s, changes in law and the definition of authority in the schools, problems of dealing with educational issues in a more unionized environment, and the pervasiveness of drug and alcohol use in the school-age population.

Adding to these difficulties is the great, and probably unnecessary, prolongation of both education and adolescence. For many decades, America's answer to the question of how to provide better education has been to require longer education. Secretaries are trained in high school but can also take two-year associate degrees and four-year baccalaureate degrees. For a physician, residency is added to internship, which comes after four years of medical school, which follows baccalaureate education, which follows twelve years of compulsory education.

While the educational process was lengthening, the onset of biological maturity was coming at an increasingly early point in that process—from high school to junior high and late elementary school. The result is millions of underachieving biological adults held captive in a secondary school system structured for children. With money, leisure time, and the encouragement of American advertisers, young people endure prolonged, pervasive, and unnecessary adolescence that encroaches unfavorably on virtually every element of secondary education as currently structured.

Since educational policy-making is highly political, achievement of significant change is problematic. There are few indications that elementary and secondary schools will be able to address effectively many of their problems. Thus, without the intervention of community colleges, many people will not receive the knowledge and skills needed to be effective citizens and workers in the twenty-first century. Community colleges are open-enrollment institutions. Unlike many baccalaureate institutions, they do not have the good fortune of tailoring courses largely to successful students, for they must deal with increasing numbers of high school dropouts and graduates whose skills are far below twelfth-grade level. These less successful students require a larger share of attention and resources; and despite community colleges' historical concern with transfer programs and with their status as collegiate institutions, they may be entering a period when they need to face more toward the secondary schools and persons for whom the educational system has not worked. But they cannot pursue this redirection in isolation. Baccalaureate institutions must acknowledge their efforts, support their missions, and recognize their own indebtedness to the two-year institutions, which make their work easier.

In the future, the community college system will be even more diverse. Its new or expanded responsibilities will include a changed interface with secondary education, renewed efforts to deal with new immigrants and educationally disadvantaged minorities, creation of a complete continuum of occupational education, increased emphasis on counseling and assessment, and greater diversity in transfer education. The task of structuring this system will be a major challenge. The strategy of simply becoming more collegiate by emphasizing transfer programs will not be the answer. Community colleges will have to expand a tradition that already embraces multiple levels of teaching on single campuses. They cannot neglect four-year college traditions but must develop a new synthesis of community college teaching that relates to the problems of the future rather than those of the past.

Changing Relations with Secondary Education

A new interface between secondary schools and higher education might include two major components. The barriers between the last two years of high school and entrance to colleges, especially to community colleges, should be ended. All relevant courses, wherever taught, should count toward a high school degree, and all college-level courses, wherever taught, should count toward a college degree. High school students who seek rewarding educational opportunities should be allowed to move without impediment between the two systems. There is already much overlap between the two. Community colleges offer many remedial courses, while advance-placement courses are taught in high school. Many occupational programs are offered by both. The last three years of high school and the first two years of college should be compressed into a four-year period. Given the duplication between high school and the first two years of college and the amount of student underachievement and dissatisfaction endemic to this country's high schools, this plan seems feasible.

Educational changes in Minnesota may herald the future. There, high school students already operate in a relatively free market of public secondary schools and colleges. Freedom of movement is limited only by the need to avoid overcrowding at some high schools. Students can seek education where they believe that they will find the greatest benefit. If they choose to attend college before receiving a high school degree, their college courses must be counted toward high school graduation requirements. Moreover, all elements of the state's educational system must now confront the policy implications that flow from a system driven by students' decisions about institutions rather than one based on compulsory attendance.

If the Minnesota plan, or some variant of it, represents the future interface between secondary school and college, how will it affect community colleges and baccalaureate institutions? First, high school enrollments will be lower and college enrollments higher. Second, elimination of duplicate courses between high school and colleges will free tax dollars for more pressing educational needs. Third, the relationship between college and high school occupational curricula will be more clearly defined. Fourth, to improve student success, colleges will have to expand their assessment and counseling functions. And, fifth, baccalaureate institutions will have to accept the "new" students who will inevitably appear on their campuses and must be prepared to offer them a full range of educational services that is currently unavailable.

These changes do not require radical alteration in the teaching approaches of community colleges, but they will demand radical reassessment and revision from most four-year institutions. Community colleges' emphases on counseling, teaching, and student success provide environments that are both supportive and challenging; they are the only kinds of environments that can succeed in meeting the new challenges of higher education.

Dealing with the Educationally Disadvantaged: New Immigration and a Renewed Commitment to the Education of Minorities

Community college teaching techniques are well suited to students with limited English proficiency and educationally disadvantaged minorities. The colleges' environments are less pressured and more supportive than those at baccalaureate institutions, while the variety of courses and range of program levels give students an array of programs tailored to their specific educational and social needs. The adaptability of the community college for these students contrasts sharply with that of four-year colleges, where programs for educationally disadvantaged minorities normally target only successful high school graduates, a minority within a minority for most ethnic groups. Nor do four-year college programs usually address the educational problems of adults.

Because of these factors, community colleges will remain the institutions attended by most educationally disadvantaged persons over eighteen years of age. They will be the educational institutions chiefly responsible for raising the skill levels of adults and young people for whom elementary and secondary education has been unsuccessful. The Puente Program, a one-year program offered in approximately twenty California community colleges for Mexican American students, illustrates the contributions that community colleges can make in serving the educationally disadvantaged. Puente students enroll in a one-year sequence of special English classes, consisting of a developmental writing course followed by a regular transfer English course. Throughout the year they are assisted by a team comprising a counselor, a mentor, and an English instructor. The specially trained counselor selects students for the programs, performs regular counseling duties, and works with the English instructor in the classroom and with the mentor in helping students develop career goals. The mentor, an older adult matched with the student in terms of personality and career interests, provides resources for some of the writing assignments and becomes a role model for the student's career path. The twelve hundred students enrolled in the program have experienced an increase in transfer rate, an improvement in grades, and a sharpening of their academic and occupational goals.

Creation of a Continuum of Occupational Education Programs

Community colleges have filled a vacuum in occupational education. Four-year institutions face major obstacles in developing comprehensive arrays of occupational programs. They customarily aim their programs at the high end of the occupational marketplace, either in preprofessional fields such as law, medicine, and dentistry or in middle-class professions such as engineering, teaching, and accounting. These are compatible with traditional liberal arts disciplines. Baccalaureate faculty have frequently dismissed or been critical of emerging mid-level technical and paraprofessional careers and have considered them inappropriate for college majors.

When developing occupational programs, community colleges generally retain a collegiate emphasis on degree programs and operate them under the traditional collegiate course structure. This framework benefits students who seek immediate employment because their status is enhanced and defined by the degree program itself. Students who wish to transfer do not discover similar benefits, however. Elitist senior college faculty frequently argue that transfer occupational programs are not collegiate and the credits should not transfer. Articulation problems occur in fields such as industrial technology, where students take most of their occupational courses at community colleges. When they transfer, they need liberal arts courses and few occupational courses. This reverses the normal collegiate pattern of taking general education in the first two years and the major in the last two years.

One solution to these articulation problems is "2 + 2" and "2 + 2 + 2" programs. A graphics program at the West Valley College in Saratoga, California, is a typical 2 + 2 program. The college's feeder high schools have reviewed courses, eliminated duplicative material, and determined the applicability of high school courses to the college's program.

The 2 + 2 + 2 programs are even more complex, since three sets of institutions are involved. An example is the business curriculum developed by West Valley, its feeder high schools, and San Jose State University. Courses at each level have been reviewed to minimize duplication and to ensure relevance to the labor market. Satisfactory performance at one level automatically guarantees admission to the next. These guarantees and the presence of personnel from both colleges on the high school campuses encourage high school students to upgrade their educational goals.

Another major problem that results when collegiate values are indiscriminately applied to occupational programs is the overly "degreed" nature of occupational programs. Many students want to take courses and quickly enter the job market. They have little interest in degree programs operating under traditional academic timetables. They need courses, both on campus and at industrial sites, that are not constrained by traditional course structures. Moreover, the marketplace changes rapidly. To some extent, community colleges are capable of effective response, certainly more so than are baccalaureate institutions, but both must be more prepared to cut red tape and quickly phase in and phase out programs.

Greater Diversity in Transfer Education

Community college transfer programs, their most collegiate functions, are also probably their most successful. Studies have repeatedly shown that community college transfers perform as well as students matriculated in senior colleges. Successful articulation agreements result from this fact. In California, for example, the University of California (UC) and the California State University (CSU) systems' annual evaluation of community college transfers invariably shows satisfactory performance. Consequently, they have developed a mutually acceptable distribution pattern for general education requirements that entails only thirty-three credit hours for the UC system and thirty-seven for the CSU system. If a community college student's general education requirements fit within this framework, he or she has met the UC or CSU general education requirements. The final step facilitating the transfer of California community college students is guaranteed admission. Each community college is in the process of completing agreements with several campuses of the UC and the CSU systems. These set out criteria for automatic admission to particular campuses on receipt of an associate degree or completion of sixty credit hours.

If the basic transfer structure is in place, community colleges need to ask themselves if they are creatively using their freedom within this structure to place a distinctive imprint on their undergraduate programs. Are they still too much under the influence of baccalaureate institutions? In the past, community colleges subordinated the individuality of their general education programs to transfer concerns. With senior colleges placing so many roadblocks in the way of transfer, community colleges have tended to develop conventional transfer programs that raise few questions at transfer time. Now they need to have the confidence to develop more innovative and substantial general education programs.

Honors programs are one way of achieving more flexibility in this area. An honors program can, in effect, become a college within a college where faculty have freedom to devise innovative programs of general education. The honors program at West Valley, for example, is based on team-taught interdisciplinary courses grouped together in a module called a *transdisciplinary unit*. In one instance, a transdisciplinary unit consists of two basic courses, Human Genetics and Mathematical Problem Solving, combined with 1- and 1.5-unit modules in library research, speech, English composition, and computer modeling. Classes are kept small, students are selected according to community college grade point averages in transfer courses, and both faculty and students are encouraged to think more creatively about general education subjects.

Transfer courses deserve serious review and reassessment from baccalaureate institutions as well. It is no longer possible to dismiss community college offerings as second-rate attempts to pander to fleeting popular demand. First, community colleges have given birth to many courses that are unparalleled in both form and content. Second, four-year faculty can no longer afford to ignore student demand by centering their attention exclusively on their own scholarly interests. There is a lesson to be learned from the community college experience with adult students, namely, that survival is linked to meeting the interests of consumers. Transfer education is the dual responsibility of community and baccalaureate institutions. It can work successfully only if the two are willing to learn from each other and to recognize that excellence in teaching is a shared endeavor.

Increased Importance of Counseling and Assessment

Community colleges, to ensure that they operate as open rather than revolving doors, emphasize counseling and assessment more than do baccalaureate institutions, which often deprecate these efforts as "coddling" or "hand-holding." Moreover, community college students look to their colleges to help them match their skills and interests with educational programs that prepare them for life. Educational counseling and assessment are essential to that task. Their importance will become even more apparent with the increasingly varied ethnic mix and higher proportion of students needing remediation. The initial step in effective teaching must be an assessment of the talents and interests of entering students, coupled with professional academic and vocational counseling. This process will help students state and assess their educational and career objectives and place themselves in courses appropriate to their skills and needs. Students will then have opportunities to profit from and pass their courses.

In California, where the current majority of students in the public schools are not members of the traditional Anglo population and where achievement levels of the public schools already lag considerably behind national norms, the need for greater emphasis in the community colleges on assessment and counseling was recognized with a multimillion dollar program called Matriculation. While no single element in the Matriculation Program is unique, the whole represents an innovative effort to deal with the problems of student access. Each major element related to student assessment, counseling, and retention was identified, and all elements were required to be part of the matriculation process at all community colleges. The state provided sufficient new funds to guarantee adequate financing.

The program has several major components: All new students are extensively tested and advised by professional counselors and are placed in orientation programs involving both academic and career counseling. Academic counseling takes place throughout the student's academic career. Placement and transfer articulation programs are available when a student is ready to seek employment or transfer to a four-year college. There is a major research and evaluation component to analyze factors that might affect students' success and to ascertain if Matriculation itself produces significant benefit to students. Finally, data systems have been improved. Counselors and researchers work with microcomputers, which are networked and connected to upgraded mainframes. New software has made information more accessible and comprehensible. Computerized testing programs, except for written essays, reduce turnaround time to a minimum.

A key factor in evaluating the results of the Matriculation Program will be the careful definition of academic success. The community college clientele is so varied in abilities and aspirations that it is crucial not to lump all students into one homogeneous mass and apply a monolithic concept of success, such as the transfer rate of all students to four-year colleges. Colleges need to identify various segments of their clientele and to develop success-rate criteria relevant to each group. Indeed, the ability to characterize accurately each major element of their student populations is critical if community colleges are to make the higher education community and the public at large more aware of their accomplishments.

Conclusion

Compared to baccalaureate institutions, community colleges have always had difficulty describing their students to the general public. There is usually no "typical student." Instead, there is great diversity in students' socioeconomic backgrounds, academic preparations, and purposes for attendance. Community college faculty and administrators have taken pride in this diversity. The best faculty members take advantage of it in the classroom because it makes their classes unique. Administrators, too, have recognized the uniqueness of their roles as they manage the educations of many distinct populations. This sense of uniqueness should now lead community college faculty and administrators to free themselves of excessive concern about how they are perceived on four-year campuses and to focus their attention on how they are perceived by their students and the public.

The task at hand is to communicate to the public an understanding of the excellent teaching and learning that takes place in community colleges.

The task confronting four-year faculty who question the validity of community college education is to realize that nationwide statistics support the contention that effective teaching and learning occur in two-year institutions and to accept that their own survival depends on working with their two-year colleagues to create better educational opportunities for America's students.

GUSTAVO A. MELLANDER is director of the Center for Community College Education at George Mason University, Fairfax, Virginia.

BRUCE ROBERTSON is director of research and planning at West Valley–Mission Community College District, Saratoga, California. He was formerly state commissioner of higher education in Missouri and assistant chancellor for research and planning at the New Jersey Department of Higher Education.

The superiority of baccalaureate institutions as centers for research and publication has long been accepted by two-year colleges. It is time for these colleges to recognize that they too make important contributions.

The Community College Unbound

George B. Vaughan

A major purpose of this volume is to examine both the positive and negative influences that baccalaureate-granting institutions have on the values and traditions of community colleges. Stated another way, how have four-year institutions shaped the culture of the community college?

One result of the influences exerted on community colleges by the four-year institutions has been, according to the editors of this volume, to bind two-year institutions to their four-year counterparts, making both community colleges and four-year institutions "prisoners of elitism." Are community colleges indeed prisoners of elitism? If so, who imprisoned them? And how? Before offering my perspective on these questions, I should point out that my assignment is not to challenge or defend the thesis as set forth by the editors but rather to relate the thesis to the research function of the community college and to its mission. Another purpose of the volume is to explore means by which the community college can achieve more stature among institutions of higher education. With these objectives in mind, I do the following in this chapter: discuss briefly my views on the "prisoner" thesis; recast my assignment and discuss the role of scholarship, rather than research, in relation to the community college professional; relate my discussion of scholarship to the positive and negative influences that four-year institutions have had and continue to have on community colleges; and explore ways by which the community college can achieve more stature among institutions of higher education.

Prisoners of Elitism

With some surprise, I find that I agree with the contention that community colleges suffer by comparison when one looks at the elite status much of society has accorded four-year institutions and denied community colleges, resulting in a form of imprisonment, or at least isolation (what, after all, is imprisonment?), for two-year institutions. The imprisonment is complex, subtle, and, in many ways, self-imposed by community college leaders. The self-imposition makes it the cruelest kind of imprisonment. Moreover, this imprisonment results largely from a failure of community colleges to emulate certain aspects of four-year institutions rather than from their capture through imitation, thus giving a perverse twist to the prisoner thesis.

How did the imprisonment come about? Certainly, the belief that four years of college are better than two still haunts community colleges and shapes their image. Many members of society and some community college faculty members believe that a "real" college should not offer remedial studies, a potpourri of continuing education courses that often lead no-where, and vocational programs nor should they work with business and industry in ways that clearly constitute training rather than education in the more traditional sense of the term. The imprisonment, then, comes from being a part of an institution that devotes much of its time, energy, and resources to operating on the edge of higher education's mainstream mission, resulting in a feeling of isolation and even inferiority. Thus, if community colleges are prisoners of elitism, it is because of their image and the self-doubts caused by that image and not because of the qualifications of community college professionals, a difference that community college leaders must understand and communicate to society in general and to other members of the higher education community in particular if the stature of community colleges is to be enhanced.

Self-concepts aside, community colleges continue to suffer from the pre-conceived notions that society has about higher education, especially regarding research. For example, I believe that much of society and far too many community college professionals suffer from the belief that, with the exception of community college faculty and administrators, all other members of the higher education community are practicing researchers. Of course, from a rational point of view, community college professionals know that most members of the higher education community do little or no research. Indeed, there is some evidence that faculty at four-year institutions are no longer willing to gloss over the failure of their colleagues to keep up with their scholarship. In a ground-breaking move, the University of Arizona recently added a section to its faculty promotion guidelines aimed at tenured professors, who have traditionally judged their younger colleagues for tenure and promotion. The addendum reads as follows: "Faculty entrusted to membership on all promotion and tenure committees shall comprise only those faculty who have met, and continue to meet, the criteria stipulated by rank in the university, college, and departmental guidelines" (Mooney, 1990, p. A15).

The Arizona case, requiring tenured full professors to *continue* to meet the criteria for their rank, is unusual and should not lead community college professionals to believe that four-year faculty are going to engage in a mass confession that many of their members neglect their scholarship, for to do so would tarnish the halo under which they now operate. In spite of isolated cases such as the University of Arizona, many community college professionals have emotionally (if not always intellectually) bought into the myth that most four-year faculty members and administrators are publishing scholars, lending support to the "prisoners of elitism" thesis. Why has the myth persisted, and, more important, why have community college professionals bought into it?

The myth persists partly because four-year faculty members encourage it, at least indirectly. For example, community college faculty members proudly proclaim that community colleges are teaching institutions, not research institutions. Of course the statement is true. But has anyone ever heard faculty members from a four-year institution, including liberal arts colleges devoted totally to teaching, proudly proclaim that they do not do research because theirs is a teaching institution? Second, the myth persists because four-year institutions—no matter how isolated, how marginal their existence, how mundane their instructional programs, how average their faculty—bask in the glow of the halo that surrounds four-year research institutions, creating the image, in the public mind at least, that if one teaches at a four-year institution, one is by definition a scholar and a researcher. Third, the great majority of community college faculty and administrators received their graduate degrees from institutions and in disciplines that emphasize research. Thus, a feeling of incompleteness (and even failure) remains with many community college faculty members who do not engage in research and are therefore failing to emulate their graduate school professors. (One wonders how many community college professionals have the image of their undergraduate professors as researchers, especially if the undergraduate work was done at an institution other than a research university. My guess is, very few.) Fourth, realizing that a minority of community college faculty and administrators engage in scholarship, including publication of their work, many community college professionals nevertheless find it easier and more convenient to hide behind the "teaching institution" claim than to be scholars and teachers rather than just teachers. Finally, and most important for this discussion, the myth persists because community college professionals have failed to explain what the role and responsibility of the community college professional should be, a role and responsibility that goes beyond teaching. The remainder of this discussion is devoted to the last point.

Recasting the Argument

Are community colleges committed to teaching over research? Of course they are. And so too are all liberal arts colleges, most state colleges, and practically all of the undergraduate divisions at even the most prestigious research institutions. Do community college faculty members fail to conduct research regularly? Yes, and so too do the majority of the faculty members teaching in American colleges and universities. Should community college professionals conduct research? The majority should not, and certainly not in the manner of the research university.

So what is the problem? The problem with many community college professionals (and indeed with much of higher education) is that they have been drawn into the age-old debate of teaching versus research, which is, I believe, the wrong debate at the wrong time. The debate of teaching versus research only serves as a smoke screen obscuring what should be the real debate for community college professionals: Can one be an outstanding teacher or administrator without also being a scholar?

By debating the issue of teaching versus research, community college professionals back themselves into a corner—imprison themselves— whereby logic dictates that they come down on the side of teaching, a stance that has historically caused the great majority of community college faculty and administrators to reject research for any number of reasons, at least for themselves. Most of them do not reject research intellectually so much as they "cool themselves out"; that is, they do not do research because community colleges are teaching institutions and therefore require no research activities by the faculty or administrators.

On the other hand, by shifting the topic to scholarship and teaching versus teaching only, we create a debate in which community college professionals should engage vigorously and continuously. For the debate is indeed compatible with and, I believe, vital to the community college mission. To shift the focus of debate from the age-old topic of research versus teaching, however, it is necessary that community colleges define and distinguish scholarship and research.

Need for a Definition

As suggested above in reference to the University of Arizona, community colleges are not the only institutions concerned with scholarship. Another example of this concern comes from Timothy S. Healy, former president of Georgetown University. He observes that "scholarship keeps the professor himself alive, gives him confidence in his exposition, and usually makes him blessedly unafraid to acknowledge ignorance or even error" (Healy, 1988). Further, Healy places the debate of scholarship versus teaching in a perspective that supports my call for scholarship among community college professionals. Observing that each spring faculty members at the nation's colleges and universities find themselves again faced with "the sharp and immemorial debate . . . about teaching and scholarship—rather, teaching *versus* scholarship," Healy concludes that "the debate is quite simply founded on a false premise.

The two activities, teaching and scholarship, are not incompatible, even less opposed. It is not true that this teaching bears no relation to research and scholarship. As a matter of fact, it seems to me that these two great works stand as cause and effect. All other goods of the university flow from its scholarship, and without it all of them are diminished, indeed suspect." Finally, Healy correctly observes that the excitement of learning, that scholarship, "is a common anchor in our profession, a given of our talk, the basis of the respect we have each for each and . . . the only solid ground on which civility can rest."

While Healy's insights are useful, he still leaves us wanting for a definition of scholarship, or even a distinction between scholarship and research, which is a shortcoming of his discussion. Perhaps the assumption is that, other than community college professionals, all of higher education has a good understanding of what constitutes scholarship. If this is the assumption, there is evidence to suggest that it is false.

Ronald W. Walters, a professor of political science at Howard University and president of the Black Faculty Congress, dramatically calls attention to the need for a definition of scholarship: "Many people in education get away with murder because they are not called upon to defend their definition of scholarship" (Vaughan, 1989b, p. 3). Another view comes from Harley L. Sachs, professor emeritus of humanities at Michigan Technological University. Sachs is troubled by the university's unwillingness to broaden its definition of what constitutes legitimate scholarship. He believes that the result is "mountains of articles of dubious scholarship and countless slipshod presentations at academic conventions" (Vaughan, 1989b, p. 3). Sachs goes on to note that universities value only those articles published in refereed journals. He believes that articles in magazines or the Sunday newspaper might well serve the profession, the university, and the community more adequately than do esoteric articles read by a few scholars.

The "mountains of articles" to which Sachs refers also concern Michael Shenefelt, a teacher of philosophy at New York University's School of Continuing Education. Shenefelt suggests that universities are now producing disposable scholarship. Referring to the over five hundred scholarly articles published on Shakespeare in 1987, Shenefelt (1989) notes that anyone reading all of the articles would have no time left for reading Shakespeare. He concludes that most of the articles are disposable, their purpose rarely being to enlighten but rather to get the author a job. One must wonder how much more valuable an article on Shakespeare in the newspaper's Sunday supplement would be. But, as Sachs points out, it probably would not enhance one's career.

Scholarship: A Definition

In Vaughan (1988), I defined scholarship and research in ways that I believe are in concert with the roles of community college professionals, both teachers and administrators. My definition of scholarship, which was carefully reviewed by a number of four-year and two-year scholars, is more inclusive than most, which often make no distinction between scholarship and research, employing the terms interchangeably.

> *Scholarship* is the systematic pursuit of a topic, an objective, rational inquiry that involves critical analysis. It requires the precise observing, organizing, and recording of information in the search for truth and order. Scholarship is the umbrella under which research falls, for research is but one form of scholarship. Scholarship results in a product that is shared with others and that is subject to the criticism of individuals qualified to judge the product. This product may take the form of a book review, an annotated bibliography, a lecture, a review of existing research on a topic, a speech that is a synthesis of the thinking on a topic. Scholarship requires that one have a solid foundation in one's professional field and that one keep up with the developments in that field.

> *Research* is a systematic, objective search for new knowledge or a new application of existing knowledge. It results in knowledge that is verifiable based on empirical data, consensus in the field, or rules of logic. Others must be able to replicate the results of the research by following the same procedures. Research is not simply the act of gathering information or collecting data in a vacuum; it builds upon previous scholarly efforts and involves the understanding of relationships among data. One must be able to draw conclusions, interpretations, or more powerful generalizations as a result of the research process [1988, p. 27].

Whether one accepts my definitions or develops new ones, the important point remains: Community colleges must grapple with what it means to be a faculty member or administrator in a community college today and in the future. One conclusion must be that if the community college is to achieve its potential and gain stature among institutions of higher education, the community college professional must understand, support, and engage in scholarship. A second conclusion is that most community college professionals should not devote a great deal of time and energy to research. But to accept or reject these conclusions, or even to debate them intelligently, one must define one's terms. Perhaps my definitions can serve as a starting point.

Failure to Promote Scholarship

Why have community colleges failed to promote scholarship? Stated another way, why is scholarship perceived as a part of the culture of four-year institutions but not as a part of the culture of community colleges?

Certainly, the lack of a definition of scholarship that is compatible with the community college mission has been an inhibiting factor, as has the smoke-screen debate of research versus teaching. Even if community college faculty and administrators agreed on a definition of scholarship, community colleges would not automatically escape the image, the imprisonment, that has resulted in their rejection of research (and failure to replace it with the broader concept of scholarship) as a legitimate undertaking for community college professionals.

Among the other reasons that community colleges have failed to place scholarship at the heart of the academic enterprise are the following: (1) Community college academic deans and presidents give little weight to the ability, either their own or that of those who report to them, to produce scholarly publications. On a scale containing seventeen items, deans and presidents ranked the ability to produce scholarly publications last for themselves and for those who report to them (Vaughan, 1990). (2) Many community college professionals have failed to link scholarship with teaching, therefore excluding scholarship from the debate of what constitutes outstanding teaching. (3) Community colleges have failed to make scholarship a part of the reward system (promotions and tenure) and therefore rarely include it as a part of faculty and administrative evaluations. And (4) until recently, scholarship had been ignored by the American Association of Community and Junior Colleges (AACJC), the national voice for the nation's two-year colleges.

Changes in the Wind

In Vaughan (1989a), I put forth the belief that scholarship is emerging as a major concern among community college professionals. Among the reasons I gave for the increased concern are the following: the revived interest in assessment of student learning, AACJC's (1988) endorsement of scholarship in its seminal report *Building Communities: A Vision for a New Century*, a policy statement issued by the AACJC Board of Directors endorsing scholarship as an integral part of the community college philosophy, and the maturing of community colleges as institutions of higher education with faculty members who are committed to teaching in these colleges rather than viewing them as stepping-stones to positions in four-year institutions.

In Spring 1989, to test my belief regarding scholarship, I surveyed eighty-six community college chief academic officers identified by their peers as leaders in their respective states. Sixty-three of the deans responded to the survey. One of the questions asked was whether the deans perceived a new awareness of the role that scholarship should play in carrying out the community college mission. Forty-nine of the respondents said that they felt there is a new awareness, nine answered no to the question, and five were not sure. In addition to surveying those deans identified as leaders, I interviewed a number of other deans, asking them about their views of scholarship. The following quotes, taken from these heretofore unpublished interview materials, give a sense of the deans' thinking on scholarship, including some views that attitudes toward it may be changing.

One dean, who voiced his strong support of scholarship, believes that it can do two things for the community college professional: "One, it can stimulate and motivate faculty to pursue excellence, and, two, I believe it can take the institution and bring it up, if you will, one notch in terms of its levels of excellence." To encourage scholarship, he promotes the use of sabbaticals for the purpose of pursuing scholarly activities. He also includes professional presentations, articles published, and other scholarly activities as a part of the evaluation process, considering them when faculty are considered for promotions in rank.

A second dean believes that community college professionals should be involved in scholarship but admits that many are not. He notes that because community colleges do not have a publish-or-perish policy, community college professionals should not be excused from pursuing scholarly activities. A third dean, who believes that community colleges have neglected scholarship because the community college's "forte has been good teaching and creating good learning situations, not doing research and publications," sees some encouraging signs in classroom research by faculty members, which is "applied and practical research as opposed to theoretical research." A fourth dean places much of the blame for a lack of scholarship on deans and presidents: "I think that most deans of instruction do not place high emphasis on scholarship. I think that is a result of our having defined ourselves as teaching institutions. We've rejected research and the kind of reward system that four-year colleges and universities have. As a result, we have lost sight of the fact that good teaching depends upon good scholarship. I think deans of instruction and presidents have been remiss in not supporting faculty in their scholarly efforts." A fifth dean believes that scholarship has been neglected because in the past community colleges were new and therefore had to put so much time and energy into defining the mission that they had none left for scholarship: "We spent so much time on [the mission], thereby missing in the end that if we do not change students intellectually, if we can't present an intellectual environment, then probably we're not going to be as successful in our role as we're expected to be." He adds that deans should be scholars but that "we're not really role models for that because we're technicians."

Is there more emphasis on scholarship today? One dean believes so: "We're constantly looking at faculty renewal, exchange programs in which we can do those things. We are also looking at the ways of getting our people published. One of the things we have found [is that] our people do a lot of writing of high caliber within our college, but it never goes anywhere, so they get no credit for it. We say that the same effort can get them published nationally" and that would mean a "reward coming back to them." Further, he believes that there is a renewed interest in scholarship because "we have to project what we're trying to tell students they should know."

Another dean gives credit to AACJC for creating a renewed interest in scholarship. Her institution has started a chapter of Phi Theta Kappa, a community college student honors society similar to Phi Beta Kappa at four-year institutions, to encourage student scholarship. The institution is considering establishing faculty chairs for outstanding teachers who are also scholars.

A dean from a Florida community college believes that external pressures have caused her state's community colleges to put more emphasis on what is taught and what is learned, and that students should be encouraged to enter college and, once in, to complete their degree requirements. She believes that there is more emphasis on accountability, resulting in greater sensitivity to scholarship. She also believes that faculty members are experiencing what it is like to teach academically strong students. Faculty are pushed by the better students "who expect a college teacher to be intellectual and have answers that go beyond the textbook," thus a new emphasis on scholarship.

If scholarship is to make significant inroads into the community college philosophy, the chief academic officers of these colleges must view scholarship as both a practical and intellectual necessity. They also must show leadership by creating a culture in which scholarship plays an important role.

Encouraging Signs

If scholarship is on the upswing in community colleges, what is being done to encourage it? A number of deans in my survey indicated that their colleges do indeed recognize and encourage scholarship. For one dean, promotion of scholarship is an important part of his role as an institutional leader:

> As my institution's academic leader, I have consistently and persistently promoted the value and necessity of scholarship. I was instrumental in establishing a system which provides for a very generous sabbatical program for faculty. In addition to the sabbatical program, I was instrumental in working with the president and board of trustees to establish a system whereby faculty, full-time and part-time, can take courses and be reimbursed for those courses. Further, we have established a generous travel budget used to urge faculty to attend conferences and special gatherings in their professional fields. Additionally, our framework for faculty evaluation includes scholarly activities as a high-priority item.

Promotion, retention, and recognition are a direct result of that high priority. This institution is unified, enthusiastic, and committed to scholarship as a pervasive ingredient absolutely necessary for the accomplishment of our mission.

As evident in the above quote, scholarship is making some inroads into the evaluation process. Another dean alludes to scholarship in relationship to promotions in rank: "For the first time, scholarship is a component of the rewards system. An evaluation of scholarship has been built into the 'promotion in rank' system. The ranking system itself is new." Similarly, a dean notes that his institution "values scholarly activities for promotion, sabbaticals, and tenure decisions, and this has made a *big* difference."

Another dean sees himself as the key to the promotion of scholarship on his campus. "I'm trying to be a role model by writing seriously about community college concerns. I, with others, am supporting faculty and administrator participation in both formal [specially designed graduate courses] and informal activities that will promote, acknowledge, and reward scholarship." Another dean notes, "I'm encouraging faculty and other administrators to write for local newspapers [and] state scholarly journals and to submit at least one article annually to a national professional journal."

A number of deans noted that their institutions reward scholarship through awards banquets and forums, released time for writing and study, summer employment for scholarly activities, attendance at conferences, and a number of other ways that encourage faculty members and administrators to engage in scholarship. Two deans noted that their institutions publish their own journals as a means of encouraging scholarship.

These examples are encouraging if one believes that scholarship should be a more integral ingredient of the community college philosophy. On the other hand, one dean sees an element of danger in an overemphasis on scholarship, for he fears that it may push the community college in a "scholarship as publish-or-perish" direction, which he believes would detract from the community college's primary mission of teaching.

Recommendations

If scholarship is to enter the debate on community college campuses in a meaningful way, then a consensus must be reached on what is meant by scholarship. For example, scholarship should not and cannot become an important consideration in the retention and promotion process until an agreement is reached on what the word means. Here I am reminded of the early days of community college development when some campuses placed a great deal of emphasis on the role of community service in the evaluation process. To my knowledge, no one ever agreed on the meaning of *community service,* and therefore it often became a "throwaway" in the evaluation process. If the same thing happens with scholarship, then the image of the community college is tarnished rather than enhanced.

Once a definition is agreed on, community college deans and presidents should work with faculty members to bring scholarship into the evaluation process. This should be done slowly, cautiously, and with the full participation of the faculty. Scholarship should be only one aspect of the evaluation process. And, as one dean cited above cautions, the community college should not be drawn into a scholarship-or-perish syndrome.

The president and chief academic officer must take the lead in making scholarship a priority for the institution. Both individuals have any number of situations in which to demonstrate their commitment to and understanding of scholarship. The academic deans should have their national organization, the National Council of Instructional Administrators, endorse the pursuit of scholarship as a worthy and necessary undertaking for the nation's community colleges. The presidents should establish on-campus climates that promote scholarly activities and make clear that the deans' activities in this area are encouraged and supported.

Scholarship should be honored on campus. This can be done in any number of ways: public recognition of scholarly accomplishments in the college bulletin, a presidential reception in honor of scholars, forums devoted to scholarship, and so on. By publicizing scholarship, the college is sending an important message to its students and to the public.

Every effort should be made to link scholarship and outstanding teaching. Classroom research is one way of combining the two. The academic officer and division chairs should take the lead in making the vital link between teaching and scholarship; faculty members should then be encouraged to engage in scholarly activities that enhance their teaching.

Finally, the college should commit financial resources to the promotion of scholarship. While attendance at professional meetings is one avenue for keeping up to date in one's field, it is not the only one. Summer study and travel are important, as is time off from teaching during the academic year.

Conclusion

Should community college professionals pursue scholarship? Can they afford to? What are the consequences if they do not? In remarks aimed at public schools, Claire Gaudiani (1987), of Academic Alliance, places the debate in perspective: "Those who spend the most time developing our children's minds are not encouraged to develop their own. Americans do not value the intellectual ability of school teachers. Our school systems make them go begging for status in the community, for time and incentive to keep up with their subjects, and for opportunities to develop new academic interests and expand old ones."

If community colleges fail to value the intellectual ability of their faculty members and administrators, fail to seek opportunities to develop new academic interests and expand old ones through scholarship, they are likely to remain "prisoners of elitism." For until community college professionals demonstrate to the rest of the higher education community and to the public in general that they are as capable of scholarship as are their four-year counterparts, neither audience will understand or appreciate the role of the community college in America. The result will be the imprisonment that comes from projecting an image in conflict with the great accomplishments of community college professionals in serving the millions of individuals whose values and needs, like those of the community college itself, are not served by baccalaureate-granting institutions. These individuals depend on community college faculty and administrators to keep alive the fires of learning that must burn ever hotter as the nation strives to serve all segments of society with the best education possible. A key to the success of the community college in the future is a commitment to scholarship. This commitment will improve the community college's image, strengthen the confidence of its faculty, enhance student learning, and loosen the bonds of elitism. For once community college professionals commit themselves to the task at hand, they quickly become among the best at what they do.

References

American Association of Community and Junior Colleges. *Building Communities: A Vision for a New Century.* A Report of the Commission on the Future of Community Colleges. Washington, D.C.: American Association of Community and Junior Colleges, 1988. 58 pp. (ED 293 578)

Gaudiani, C. "Local Communities of Inquiry: Penn's Academic Alliance Program." *Weekly Log* (Center for Liberal Arts, University of Virginia, Charlottesville), Mar. 13–27, 1987.

Healy, T. S. " 'Wrastling' at the University." *Higher Education and National Affairs,* 1988, *36,* 7.

Mooney, C. J. "U. of Arizona Puts Limits on Who May Evaluate Professors for Promotion." *Chronicle of Higher Education,* Jan. 17, 1990, pp. A15–A16.

Shenefelt, M. "Disposable Scholarship." *Washington Post,* Sept. 12, 1989, p. A21.

Vaughan, G. B. "Scholarship in Community Colleges: The Path to Respect." *Educational Record,* 1988, *69* (2), 26–31.

Vaughan, G. B. "A New Wind 'A Blowing." *Community, Technical, and Junior College Times,* June 20, 1989a, p. 2.

Vaughan, G. B. *Scholarship: The Community College's Achilles' Heel.* Virginia Community Colleges Association, Occasional Papers, no. 1. N.p.: Virginia Community College Association, 1989b. 22 pp. (ED 313 081)

Vaughan, G. B. *Pathway to the Presidency: The Community College Deans of Instruction.* Washington, D.C.: American Association of Community and Junior Colleges, 1990. 288 pp. (ED 318 526)

GEORGE B. VAUGHAN is professor of education leadership at the University of Florida, Gainesville.

Baccalaureate institutions have traditionally assumed control of the articulation process. Community colleges must become equal partners in this process.

Establishing Equality in the Articulation Process

Roger J. Barry, Phyllis A. Barry

Recent books such as Brint and Karabel's (1989) *The Diverted Dream* criticize community colleges for sending so few students on to baccalaureate degrees. Members of the public frequently ask why community college credits "won't transfer," and community college students who have completed technical coursework that is as demanding as upper-division and graduate work at four-year colleges and universities are angry when this work does not count toward a baccalaureate degree. Yet, community colleges are not the sole or primary cause of the dissatisfaction. The traditions, values, and methods of baccalaureate education have negatively influenced the community college transfer function, much to the frustration of community college administrators and faculty.

The community colleges are truly "prisoners of elitism" as they struggle to perform the transfer function in creative and effective ways. Part of the reason for their struggle can be traced to one of the origins of the community college. Prior to the community college movement, junior colleges offered the first two years of the baccalaureate degree. These precursors to the community college fixed in the public's mind the idea that the primary function of community colleges was to prepare people to transfer to baccalaureate institutions.

Early community college leaders, anxious to prove that community colleges were truly collegiate institutions, did little to dispel this perception of baccalaureate faculty, administrators, and the public. Community college liberal arts faculty, products of the baccalaureate system, designed transfer courses and curricula to be similar to the courses that they had taken. Faculty and administrators in baccalaureate colleges judged community colleges by the criteria used in baccalaureate colleges and assumed that the successful community college student transferred and completed a baccalaureate degree. Few baccalaureate faculty understood or appreciated the other facets of the community college mission such as technical education, work force training and retraining, and community and continuing education.

Effective transfer, however, requires that community colleges articulate with baccalaureate institutions. The diversity of baccalaureate colleges in the United States makes articulation a challenge because colleges require their own selected courses for graduation and may refuse to grant transfer credit for essentially the same courses offered at other institutions. Baccalaureate colleges, proud of their diversity and autonomy, have historically opposed bureaucratic forces that sought consistency among colleges in general education requirements and course content.

Baccalaureate colleges often fought centralized direction while community colleges sought some degree of commonality of general education and specific courses so that their students could successfully transfer. As a result of these constraints, community colleges have frequently become "prisoners of elitism" as they have attempted to perform their transfer function.

Definitions

The following terms are commonly used in discussing articulation, particularly in regard to transfer between two- and four-year institutions.

Collegiate Function. Cohen and Brawer (1987, p. 5) describe the community college's collegiate function as "an amalgam of liberal arts curriculum and efforts to promote student transfer. It is most pronounced in the colleges' activities designed first to provide a general education, then to pass students through to senior institutions." This fundamental mission of the community college includes the transfer function, which is defined as the movement of students from one institution of higher education to another. The transfer function requires attention to "the mechanics of credit, course, and curriculum exchange" (Kintzer and Wattenbarger, 1985, p. iii).

Articulation. Articulation is the "systematic coordination between an educational institution and other educational institutions and agencies designed to ensure the efficient and effective movement of students among those institutions and agencies, while guaranteeing the students' continuous advancement in learning" (Ernst, 1978, p. 32).

General Education and Liberal Arts. In most cases, general education is the liberal arts component of the associate and baccalaureate degrees. Included here are courses intended to impart knowledge, intellectual concepts, and attitudes common to educated people.

Historical Development of the Transfer Function

The transfer function has always been considered fundamental to the community college mission. The junior college, conceptualized as providing the first two years of a university education, was one of the antecedents of the modern community college. Many states created their community college systems to serve as feeder institutions to a stratified college and university system. The four-year colleges and universities benefited from having locally based institutions expand educational access and sort students in terms of their academic potential.

The transfer function of the community college has always been the part of the mission that people use as a measure of a "real" college. The founders of the community college movement believed that the credibility of their institutions depended on the ability of students to transfer to four-year colleges with a minimum of problems. Community college leaders today, however, regard the transfer function as a crucial part of their mission, but not necessarily more important than other assigned responsibilities such as technical education, work force training and retraining, and community and continuing education.

Enrollments of students in transfer programs dominated community colleges until the early 1970s. Then, liberal arts and general education enrollments shifted downward through the 1980s (57 percent in 1970-1971 to 28 percent in 1984-1985). The decline of transfer students is attributed to the rapid increase of enrollments in technical programs, a decline in high school enrollments, and increased competition from four-year colleges. The recent upsurge in transfer students is due, in part, to increased admission selectivity at universities, significant increases in tuition at universities, and an increase in the number of high school graduates and adults who are not prepared for university admission.

The success of the transfer function across the United States has had more to do with strong state leadership and the resulting commitment to transfer success than to any issues of quality of instruction or knowledge gained by students. The transfer function is alive and well and works best in states where formal articulation-transfer agreements are mandated. It functions most poorly where an absence of state direction and leadership forces the colleges and universities to work out the transfer function among themselves.

The reason for the weak transfer function when there is a lack of state leadership relates to the perceptions of the universities and their faculties and to the lack of a bureaucratic mechanism to make the transfer function work. State leadership became involved in transfer negotiations in Florida, Illinois, Georgia, and Texas in 1971. By 1973, at least thirty-two states had articulation-transfer agreements in which state agency policy or legal mandate was the driving force.

In Illinois, during the late 1960s and the 1970s, the staff of the Illinois Community College Board hosted annual meetings between representatives of the state community colleges and universities. Conferences were sponsored for faculty to develop discipline-based transfer agreements. These were successful in mathematics and agriculture but less successful or unsuccessful in disciplines with less structured curricula. Over time a successful system of course-by-course articulation was worked out between colleges and universities, allowing for significant variations between universities. By the 1980s, most of the state universities agreed to the statewide articulation agreement giving junior-level status to transfer associate degree graduates and accepting their lower-division general education coursework for the universities' general education requirements.

In Ohio, on the other hand, the Board of Regents was assigned a coordinating function rather than a policy function; as a result, it was only with action by the legislature in 1989 that the board again took up the issue of transfer and articulation. Without a two-year transfer advocate at the state level to press the issues associated with statewide transfer policies, each two-year college has had to negotiate with receiving universities to accept transfer students, but the success of those negotiations depended solely on the structures and attitudes of the receiving universities.

Some Ohio universities provide opportunities for students graduating from two-year colleges with transfer-oriented associate degrees to enter with junior-level status; others offer an opportunity for two-year students to transfer after completing a general education core. In addition, a few have developed transfer catalogues that show course equivalencies between two-year colleges and the universities. Some Ohio research universities have essentially no office with which to negotiate a transfer agreement; individual departments and colleges must be contacted separately, and the agreements expire with changes in personnel. Consequently, students in Ohio often find transferring from two-year colleges to state four-year colleges (even within the same institution) cumbersome, fraught with misinformation, frustrating, and demeaning. In particular, transfer of credit is consistently ranked high by students and parents among areas of greatest dissatisfaction. Administrators of two-year colleges in Ohio consider the state's system one of the most backward in the nation in dealing with articulation and transfer.

Successful Articulation Programs

There are three types of articulation programs sponsored by state governments (Moore, 1989): (1) formal and legally based policies, which are preservative and defined in state law with mandated mechanisms in place to ensure compliance; (2) state system policies, which result from statewide articulation-transfer agreements negotiated between two-year and four-year college representatives and formalized in state policy, with mandatory institutional compliance; and (3) voluntary agreements, which are statewide articulation-transfer agreements negotiated between two-year and four-year college representatives, with voluntary institutional compliance. The highest transfer rates have been in the states where the articulation-transfer agreements have a legislative basis, such as Florida, Missouri, Texas, Washington, and Rhode Island. Illinois, California, Maryland, New Jersey, and Arizona have state system policies. Michigan, Pennsylvania, Kentucky, and Minnesota have voluntary agreements. Ohio and Massachusetts are examples of states that have vague early legislation encouraging articulation and transfer, but few formal agreements exist and little work is done to keep them up to date.

University Faculty Perceptions of Two-Year Institutions. University faculty contend that many community college courses, though seemingly comparable based on catalogue descriptions, lack the breadth and depth of subject matter taught in the first two years of a baccalaureate institution. In addition, they claim that because community colleges have open-admission policies and substantial remediation programs, the courses at the associate degree level are "watered down" to accommodate limited academic abilities. Baccalaureate faculty also contend that they have no effective way of judging quality of courses or curricula at community colleges. In essence, they live in fear of loss of faculty autonomy in the determination of course equivalencies and student admission criteria.

The results are that without strong state leadership and appropriate mechanisms to protect students, baccalaureate faculty assess transfer equivalencies based on their subjective perceptions of and limited experiences with community colleges; their evaluations are thus erratic and inconsistent. Faculty who are knowledgeable about community colleges believe that there is no significant difference in courses, whereas others assume that what students learn in community colleges could not compare in course content to what they teach.

Community College Faculty Perceptions. When the community college was a relatively new institution and its faculty believed that their courses had to be similar to those that they had taken as students, they sought approval of their courses from their baccalaureate peers. Time and a better appreciation of the success of the community college mission and students have brought pride and satisfaction to community college faculty as master teachers. Increasingly, community college faculty believe that because they have an exclusive teaching mission, they are preparing students for upper-division work more thoroughly than are either the inexperienced teaching assistants at four-year institutions who teach many of the freshman-level courses or the distracted faculty at these institutions who prefer research and specialized subject areas to freshman and sophomore courses.

Today, most community college faculty contend that their courses are every bit as rigorous as comparable university courses. They believe that small classes, individualized attention, and dedication to pedagogy qualify them as master teachers who help a significant number of students correct academic deficiencies. This belief has been reinforced by the successes of former students who have transferred to four-year institutions.

Transfer Function Successes

Community college students who transfer after completing associate degrees or a significant amount of satisfactory coursework are as successful as native baccalaureate students in academic performance and persistence toward four-year degrees. Recent studies in Florida and Washington indicate that community college transfer students who completed bachelor's degrees had performance and persistence records similar to students who matriculated in baccalaureate institutions.

Students who complete only a few hours of credit at community colleges and then transfer should not be included in comparisons of transfer success. The only students for which community colleges can fairly be held responsible are those who complete requirements for associate degrees with acceptable grade point averages. Yet, students who have taken a few hours at a community college and then transferred and performed poorly are often identified as community college transfer students. In reality, these students were probably ill-advised to enter four-year colleges, where fewer student support services are available. Their failures should not be attributed to inadequacies in the two-year institutions.

There is evidence that the overall grade point averages of many transfer students drop by one-half of a point during their first upper-division year, a phenomenon known as "transfer shock." In most cases, however, the students recover and earn grade point averages comparable to native baccalaureate students at the time of graduation (Kintzer and Wattenbarger, 1985). The irony is that some elitists view this temporary drop in grade point averages as proof of the limitations of community colleges, when in fact it may suggest as much or more about inadequacies in instruction and support services in baccalaureate institutions.

One of the great successes of the community college, which is frequently misunderstood when students transfer, is its approach to curriculum design and special services for students. Community college faculty have frequently taken a different route from that of their colleagues in four-year colleges by designing courses to fit the unique needs of the students. Often, courses are assigned a higher number of credit hours than are offered for identical courses at four-year colleges. The purpose is to give students more time to develop their skill levels so that they can compete with their four-year-college counterparts. For example, accounting classes often require four contact hours at the community college instead of the three hours required at a university. Community colleges may also require students to take the laboratory portions of science classes in addition to the lecture sections so that students are ensured "hands-on" laboratory experience and reinforcement. Most successful community colleges also insist that students be assessed prior to entering certain courses in order to ensure that the students have the basic reading, writing, critical thinking, and mathematics skills and knowledge needed for academic success. To elitists, these course offerings and requirements suggest incompetent students, but to those who understand the concept of open admissions and have witnessed its achievements, they are the essentials that help students fulfill their academic aspirations in both two- and four-year collegiate endeavors.

Another accusation leveled against the community colleges is that the faculty do not actively encourage students to transfer to particular majors because they themselves lack strong associations with their own disciplines. It is true that the primary concern of community college faculty is not to advance the disciplines. Instead, they focus their attention on what is appropriate to teach in those disciplines that will advance their students' general education. These faculty members recognize that classes cannot be taught as if all students are potential majors. The result is that community college faculty frequently better understand and more strongly support the concept of general education than do their research-oriented colleagues at the four-year colleges. They are interested in the pedagogy of teaching, which involves knowing how to assess student learning styles as well as how to develop new and challenging strategies for effective teaching. Writing-across-the-curriculum and thinking-across-the-curriculum, along with significant reflection on what constitutes an appropriate general education curriculum, have been strongly supported by community college faculty.

Nevertheless, the task of matching these community college interests with four-year general education requirements for transfer students has been a major problem. The failure of community colleges in their attempts to preserve the transfer function and yet to design curricula appropriate for their students derives from concern that courses will not transfer successfully. The first priority of many community colleges has been to assure students that courses designed to transfer will truly do so, with four-year college faculty as the final arbiters of what transfers. The problem is that elitism too often triumphs, for many baccalaureate faculty have limited knowledge and understanding of the demands placed on academe by the workplace because their exclusive focus is on their disciplines and research.

For example, community college faculty realize that computer literacy is appropriate for students. Arguments about what constitutes computer literacy, ranging from theoretical knowledge of computer languages to knowledge of practical computer applications, have been held in the meetings of most community college curriculum committees. Nevertheless, concern that a practical course design might not transfer has slowed the establishment of computer literacy as a general education skill requirement at community colleges. Similarly, an Illinois community college decided that a course in health education was important enough to make a general education requirement. That course transferred to the nearby regional university as a graduation requirement for the baccalaureate degree; however, the same course was not accepted for transfer at the flagship university in the state.

The task facing community college leaders and faculty is to seize the initiative and devise effective means of educating their baccalaureate colleagues about the substance and quality of community college curricula. Too often they have allowed baccalaureate institutions to dominate decisions about transfer. This domination has occurred in part because baccalaureate accrediting agencies insist on constituencies in curriculum and because the public believes that community colleges should offer courses and programs similar to those in the four-year colleges. Since most students do not want to foreclose the option for transfer at some time, they are reluctant to take courses for which transfer credit will not be awarded.

The baccalaureate colleges' review of community college courses and curricula for the purpose of transfer has encouraged a general consistency of curricula in institutions that engage in the transfer process. Introductory courses in English, geography, sociology, psychology, and history are quite similar at both four-year and community colleges, and community college faculty are sensitive to the issue of rigor and strive to ensure that their students possess the same knowledge base of students at the four-year colleges. Associations with four-year colleges have provided community college faculty with opportunities to interact with colleagues from their own disciplines, and these interactions have enhanced both the disciplines and the teaching process.

Unfortunately, however, the negative effects of the baccalaureate institutions' influence may outweigh the positive. Community college faculty often have their creativity stifled. The design of discipline-specific courses is encouraged because it is the norm in four-year institutions, even though these courses may not work well for either two- or four-year students. And eager to meet baccalaureate criteria for transfer courses, community colleges frequently overlook the more pressing needs of students, society, and the work force.

Excessive concern with pleasing baccalaureate institutions discourages community college faculty from introducing courses that are different from those taught at the four-year colleges, and truly innovative general education concepts that could be of significant value are forever lost. Moreover, because the first two years of the community college transfer curriculum are almost exclusively general education, there is an excellent opportunity to experiment with the integration of knowledge; yet, transfer requirements from discipline-dominated baccalaureate colleges make this experimentation almost an impossibility.

The misplaced and misguided elitism of many four-year college educators discourages students and wastes taxpayers' money. Students who wish to transfer are often required to repeat courses or are denied credit for legitimate courses based on uninformed or petty academic decisions, usually made without an examination of course outlines or requirements from the community colleges where the students were enrolled.

Summary

Community colleges are prisoners of elitism with little chance of escape. Community colleges are also the most successful innovation in higher education in the second half of the twentieth century. This success is in the provision of access to higher education to the citizens of this nation. Yet, in spite of their success, they must tolerate criticism, often heavy-handed, of their combination of technical training and liberal arts transfer programs within the same institutions.

Community colleges are prisoners of their origins as junior colleges, and prisoners of elitist university faculty who understand little beyond their disciplines or have limited understanding of the need to integrate knowledge through an effective general education curriculum. They are prisoners because universities and their faculties waste taxpayers' money and students' time with ineffective and poorly managed articulation agreements unless mandated to do otherwise by the power of the state.

Community college administrators and faculty must lobby for and demand strong, state-mandated articulation agreements so that they can negotiate on an equal basis with universities. Community college administrators and faculty must educate university faculty about the community college mission so that they understand the community college role in higher education. Community colleges must develop effective measures of the numbers of students who transfer or are expected to transfer and must then assess their own effectiveness in meeting the transfer mission.

References

Brint, S., and Karabel, J. *The Diverted Dream: Community Colleges and the Promise of Educational Opportunity in America, 1900–1985.* New York: Oxford University Press, 1989.

Cohen, A. M., and Brawer, F. B. *The Collegiate Function of Community Colleges: Fostering Higher Learning Through Curriculum and Student Transfer.* San Francisco: Jossey-Bass, 1987.

Ernst, R. J. "Articulation: A Working Definition." *Community College Review,* 1978, 5 (4), 32–34.

Kintzer, F. C., and Wattenbarger, J. L. *The Articulation/Transfer Phenomenon: Patterns and Directions.* Horizons Issues Monograph Series. Washington, D.C.: American Association of Community and Junior Colleges, 1985. 85 pp. (ED 257 539)

Moore, A. "Background Paper for the State Commission on Articulation and Transfer." Unpublished manuscript prepared for the Ohio Board of Regents, 1989.

ROGER J. BARRY is dean of Clermont College, a branch campus of the University of Cincinnati.

PHYLLIS A. BARRY is assistant dean of evening and continuing education at the University of Cincinnati.

Community colleges have borne the brunt of criticism about diminishing transfer rates. Accreditation bodies, as well as baccalaureate institutions, must also share in the task of encouraging academic persistence.

Accreditation and Transfer: Mitigating Elitism

Carolyn Prager

As pressure mounts on two-year institutions to promote the transfer of their students, especially minority students, to four-year programs, it is time that we examine the relationship between accreditation and transfer. While this chapter is about accreditation and transfer, it is also about elitism, negligence, and irresponsibility. The elitists are the critics who maintain that diminishing transfer rates from two- to four-year institutions are a result of function rather than structure, the function and fault being two-year education. The negligent are the accreditors who ignore the transfer fray while defining conditions hostile to student progress from two- to four-year programs. The irresponsible are those of us who hesitate to engage the accreditation community in examination of its current contribution, however unintentional, to the transfer malaise.

Response to the Transfer Malaise

The diminished flow of students from two-year college transfer tracks to the senior colleges has prompted the intervention of those outside of higher education into what were previously seen as institutional issues. For almost three decades, the assertion that community colleges in and of themselves depress the academic expectations, educational persistence, and economic potential of their students has dominated the criticism of "outsiders" (Oromaner, 1984). Seen from their perspective, attendance at a community college in and of itself reduces baccalaureate degree aspirations, paradoxically decreasing rather than increasing the educational opportunity of the very populations that the community college has come to serve.

Further, community colleges are seen to achieve these negative ends by shunting students into vocational programs (Pincus, 1986).

The overall qualitative and quantitative diminution of transfer students from the two-year college is actually the result of complex social trends and public policies. One trend is the unbalanced distribution of working class and minority students to community colleges (Karabel, 1986), which has led to the expansion of compensatory and career curricula at the expense of traditional transfer studies (Baron, 1982; Cohen and Brawer, 1989; Kissler, 1982; Knoell, 1982; Lombardi, 1979). This situation is an outcome of public policy designating community colleges as open-access institutions. The trend toward vocationalization throughout higher education has led to a reordering of college curricula at the expense of general education. This de-emphasis of general education has particularly important implications for the growing number of students enrolled in career programs—as opposed to transfer programs—who aspire to obtain baccalaureate degrees and actually do transfer either upon graduation or after entering the work force.

The best available evidence suggests that as many as 75 percent of so-called vocational-technical students hope to pursue four-year degrees (Hunter and Sheldon, 1980), and at least 50 percent of all transferees now come from the so-called nonacademic track (Cohen and Brawer, 1989; Bader-Borel, 1984). The "nontransfer" associate in applied science degree appears to generate the largest number of transfer students, which in turn may be one of the major factors underlying the perceived decline in transfer student performance (Kissler, 1982). In light of the number of two-year career program students who go on to four-year curricula, it may no longer be even meaningful to talk of liberal arts and science versus vocational tracks as if one were for transfer and the other were not (Prager, 1988).

In response largely to social demands for access to and equity in higher education for minorities, government agencies and private foundations such as the Fund for the Improvement of Postsecondary Education and the Ford Foundation have made significant efforts to counter the "devaluation of transfer" (Bernstein, 1986). Typically, in the Ford-funded Urban Community Colleges Transfer Opportunities Program, colleges have undertaken activities such as assisting high school students in obtaining skills requisite to success in college before matriculation, strengthening their general education curricula, improving course and program articulation with senior institutions, improving student support transfer services, and developing sophisticated information and tracking systems. With some exceptions, however, most transfer-enhancing projects are geared toward improving the number and performance of transfer students on the liberal arts and science track. Advocates of this approach maintain that it represents a significant attempt to reaffirm community college links in higher education through restoration of the transfer connection (Palmer, 1987).

Whether or not such efforts will materially alter the quantity and quality of the community college transfer student remains to be seen, given the recency of these new transfer initiatives.

Structural Causes of the Transfer Malaise

There are other, more deeply rooted structural causes of the transfer malaise, however, that are best addressed from *within* higher education by the accreditation community, a potentially powerful change agent in American higher education. Three factors in particular are prominent sources of trouble, each of which is difficult to address at the institutional level because current accreditation guidelines not only do not encourage attention to them but also frequently discourage their consideration. The first factor is the absence of a strong mandate to the senior institutions to articulate baccalaureate and associate degree curricula in ways that facilitate the transfer of students from two-year colleges, in similar programs, without the loss of considerable credit.

The second factor is the absence of a strong mandate to employ occupationally specific faculty who hold more than baccalaureate or associate degrees in career programs at the two- and four-year colleges. Although little if any research has been done to corroborate the claim, common sense suggests that faculty members with only an associate degree—or even only a baccalaureate degree—may not present a strong role model of academic attainment and may not enunciate strong convictions to their students regarding the importance of still higher education.

The third factor is the absence of a strong general education mandate in career curricula, arguably the most important factor in enhancing students' educational mobility. The general education issue should not be dismissed by protesting that the exigencies of specialized professional coursework prohibit more liberal arts and science courses in the curriculum. The issue may not be so much about curriculum distribution as it is about pedagogy and focus, that is, not so much a question of what is taught than of how it is taught (Cohen and Brawer, 1989). By ignoring the integration of computation, communications, and analytical skills into course content, many technical courses, especially those that are competency-based, simply fail to reinforce the acquisition of general education skills important to educational mobility. In the present accreditation context, however, enrichment of the content and delivery of technical programs in order to develop their transfer potential is difficult to achieve at the institutional level.

Given present realities, accreditation bodies have the potential to foster structural changes by focusing more attention on intercollegiate program articulation, on general education standards, and on faculty qualifications in ways that enhance transfer possibilities and outcomes. Both regional and specialized agencies have this potential. The former help define institutional standards and outcomes, which can and should include better delivery of those elements deemed important to transfer education, including programmatic articulation. The latter directly or indirectly set the minimum criteria for a program's content, pedagogy, faculty, articulation, and professional relationships, all factors that contribute to its transfer value.

Scope of Accreditation

The numbers of those who accredit and those who are accredited have grown enormously in the last decade. Colleges with career-oriented curricula tend to maintain multiple accreditation relationships. Indeed, because of the presence of vocational programs, community colleges probably have a larger number of accreditation relationships relative to the number of programs than does any other sector of higher education, except for technical institutes. By extension, if accreditation has any bearing on transferability of students and courses, then its bearing is greatest on the community college because of the sector's sheer number of accreditation relationships.

Community college participation in accreditation shows no signs of decreasing. On the contrary, the sector will probably become more involved than ever before in accreditation relationships given the ever-increasing proliferation of specialized accreditation bodies. According to Kells and Parrish (1986), there has been an 81.2 percent volume increase since 1978 in allied health program accreditation alone at regionally accredited institutions of higher education. Of the ten highest ranked accreditors in terms of volume, four are directly involved in the evaluation of associate degree programs: Accreditation Board for Engineering and Technology, National League for Nursing, Committee on Allied Health Education and Accreditation's (CAHEA's) Joint Review Committee for Education in Radiologic Technology, and CAHEA's National Accrediting Agency for Clinical Laboratory Sciences (for medical laboratory technology). In addition, two out of the top ten, the National League for Nursing and the American Assembly of Collegiate Schools of Business, evidence policies and practices with consequences for community college transfer because of their accreditation policies and practices at the baccalaureate level.

Policies and Practices: Specialized Agencies

In my review of the policies and practices of five of the ten more prolific accreditation bodies, I found that these agencies pay scant attention to structural elements that could bolster the transfer function. These elements are (1) encouragement of four-year institutions to articulate their programs to two-year college programs and their graduates, (2) encouragement of all colleges to employ occupationally specific faculty with more than an associate or baccalaureate degree, and (3) encouragement of all colleges to truly integrate general and career education. This review was based not only on the official guidelines of the agencies but also on their responses to a written survey that I conducted in 1988. Respondents, either agency directors or designees, were queried about (1) the minimum degree requirements for the chief academic administrator and specialty faculty in the programs evaluated by their respective organizations, (2) the number and distribution of general education courses and credits required for the associate and/or baccalaureate degrees, (3) if and how the evaluation process determined that program instructors provided opportunities for the reinforcement of oral, written, and analytical proficiencies, and (4) whether or not the accreditation body had adopted or planned to adopt criteria that foster student transfer and programmatic articulation. The five agencies are reviewed below.

National Accrediting Agency for Clinical Laboratory Sciences (NAACLS). According to NAACLS (1986), an associate degree program preparing medical laboratory technicians (MLTs) is two academic years in length. The availability of medical technologist (MT) baccalaureate degree programs does not ease the problem of transfer and articulation because of the imbalance between associate and baccalaureate program requirements. NAACLS (1986), for example, leaves the scope of all general education in associate degree programs, including natural science, mathematics, communications, and behavioral science—courses and credits unspecified—to the discretion of the teaching institution. By contrast, pre- or corequisites for the MT baccalaureate degree program include general chemistry, organic and/or biochemistry, general biological sciences, microbiology, immunology, and college-level mathematics. The incompatibility of the associate and baccalaureate degree curricula is obvious.

Although not noted in NAACLS (1986), agency officials responded that associate and baccalaureate degree programs are required to demonstrate evidence of articulation efforts. However, the disparity between preparation to become an MLT versus an MT does not make the transition between the two smooth for those coming from two-year programs, unless these programs are far more rigorously constructed by the sponsoring institution than is required by the accreditation association. Students who might choose to transfer into a baccalaureate degree program other than in medical technology are, of course, at an equal or even greater disadvantage, depending on the extent to which their institutionally determined curriculum sequence has provided sufficient general education to realistically call their movement from two- to four-year education "transfer."

The minimum requirement for the chief academic administrator and the faculty in an NAACLS-approved MLT program is a four-year degree. A master's degree is deemed "highly desirable" (NAACLS, 1986, p. 2) for the program director. However, according to data derived from the agency's listing of MLT programs at 150 or so regionally accredited institutions awarding the associate degree, approximately 28 percent of the program directors had no academic degree whatsoever or one less than the baccalaureate. Approximately 58 percent had the master's and 11 percent the doctorate. Of the sixty or so programs at senior institutions, about 26 percent of the directors had no academic degree or less than the baccalaureate, and about 57 percent had the master's. In other words, the hiring patterns for MLT programs located in community colleges and for those in four-year colleges, universities, or medical schools are relatively similar.

Joint Review Committee on Education in Radiologic Technology (JRCERT). In common with several other allied health fields, the educational standards for radiology personnel build in limited expectations for the academic preparation of technical faculty and academic accomplishments of students in ways that inhibit the latter's movement from the first to the second degree. Radiation therapist technologist (RTT) and radiographer programs also illustrate problems of program certification common to multiple-entry-level professions. According to JRCERT (1981), RTT programs may be of twelve or twenty-four months' duration, while radiographer programs consist of two years of full-time study. Either may be established in community and junior colleges, senior colleges and universities, hospitals, clinics, autonomous radiation oncology centers, medical schools, or postsecondary vocational-technical schools and institutions.

JRCERT (1981, p. 2) requires that RTT and radiographer curricula include technical and related "competencies and learning objectives" or "content areas" such as medical terminology, radiobiology, radiographics, radiation oncology, radiation physics, clinical dosimetry, patient care, and medical ethics and law, depending on the different professional orientations. They do not set any requirement for general education, except indirectly by maintaining that graduates must demonstrate competence in the practice of oral and written communication and performance of basic mathematical functions. For radiographers, JRCERT (1983, p. 3) defines oral and written communication as "medical communication," hardly the English or composition commonly taught in the first two years of undergraduate instruction. The committee also requires that students demonstrate an awareness of patient physical and emotional stress patterns and an ability to interact with patients and families without any recommendation for coursework in the social and behavioral sciences that contribute to such professional facility. General education coursework, if any, is left to the discretion of the sponsoring institution with the proviso that a degree, if awarded, have requirements consistent with other degrees awarded by the institution.

Individuals may qualify to direct a certified RTT or radiographer education program at a college or elsewhere in one of three different ways, none of which requires a graduate degree. JRCERT (1981, 1983) states that a director must have taught for a minimum specified period in an accredited program and must have a baccalaureate degree with a minimum of two years of professional experience, or an associate degree with a minimum of four years of such experience, or *no degree* and a minimum of five years of related experience. Individuals may qualify to teach clinical courses with only the professional credential and two years of professional experience.

As with other allied health programs, collegiate institutions in practice accept program directors within the full range of permissible qualifications, despite what one would expect to be a higher institutional standard for faculty. According to data derived from the JRCERT's list of accredited programs, five of the fifteen two-year college-affiliated programs for the RTT, for example, were headed by individuals with no listed college degrees, one by an individual with the associate, seven with the baccalaureate, and one with the master's. Of the thirty-seven programs affiliated with four-year colleges or universities, thirteen were headed by individuals with no college degrees, fifteen with the baccalaureate, and nine with the master's.

JRCERT does not involve itself in questions of academic articulation but does ask that two-year programs counsel students about career mobility in their chosen fields and ensuing educational requirements. In a profession that sets very low levels of minimum educational attainment for its own professoriate and low standards of general education for its students, associate degree program graduates will most likely encounter academic constraints on their ability to transfer into and succeed in programs leading to the baccalaureate, especially since they are apt to find themselves in other than radiologic programs of upper-level study because of limited transfer options within the field.

National League for Nursing (NLN) (Associate Degree). Theoretically, NLN has eased the way for academic and career mobility in the nursing profession to a degree absent in most health care fields through its insistence on higher faculty qualifications and more substantial general education coursework. Indeed, NLN (1982b) endorsed movement within the profession, charging institutions with the responsibility for developing curricula that enable individuals to change career goals, defined as advancement from one type of nursing practice to another.

NLN supports its philosophical position on mobility with academic standards for faculty and curricula that are typically regarded as collegiate. NLN (1982a) requires that both the program director and faculty have master's degrees with a major in nursing (except for program directors appointed prior to 1983, whose qualifications are individually subject to NLN scrutiny). Faculty members are also required to demonstrate continued improvement of their nursing and teaching expertise through academic study, clinical practice, and other appropriate activities.

NLN (1982a) calls for 40 percent or more of general education in the total credit allocation at the associate degree level. The recommendation that nursing philosophy and objectives guide the selection of general education courses is tempered somewhat by the requirement that nursing students have the opportunity to register in general education courses with students from other majors. Although not specifically noted in NLN (1982a) or in guidelines for site visits, external evaluation teams examine samples of student work for evidence that instructors take into account both oral and written communication skills in technical classrooms, laboratories, and clinical assignments.

NLN has not yet formally adopted a policy encouraging two- to four-year program articulation, despite its strong position statements on educational mobility and the award of competency-based credit for nursing knowledge. NLN has thereby provided the theoretical framework for student passage from the associate to the baccalaureate degree, even if in practice the institutional requirements for the two degrees are often so disparate that in many cases community and senior college curricula are not parallel.

Accreditation Board for Engineering and Technology (ABET). Historically, associate degree programs in the engineering technologies have led to employment upon graduation and, more recently, to both employment and transfer into articulated programs, many developed on the 2 + 2 model. Despite formal classification of engineering technology programs as career programs, ABET's accreditation criteria reflect the dual nature of what are essentially dedicated transfer track curricula at the two-year level. The specified standards for general education serve to ease transfer. Almost 40 percent of the sixty-four minimum credits required for the associate degree are in mathematics (beginning with college algebra), basic science as distinguished from technical science or computer programming, and social science and/or humanities and communications (the latter for at least six credits). There are, however, slight curriculum imbalances between lower- and upper-level programs caused by the associate degree's inherent duality in providing for both employment and transfer. The associate degree, for example, requires only nine credits total in social science, humanities, and communications, compared to the twenty-four credits required for the baccalaureate. As a result, depending on how the twenty-four credits are distributed in the first two years of the undergraduate curriculum at a four-year school, students transferring into their junior years may find themselves with less of a general education background than native juniors.

ABET requires that a majority of the two-year program faculty have master's degrees in the same field as, or one complementary to, the subject being taught, as well as appropriate industrial experience. Registration as a professional engineer, architect, or surveyor is accepted in lieu of a master's degree. Technical skills faculty may represent only a small fraction of the technical faculty. They are not expected to have advanced degrees but, according to ABET (n.d., p. 9), are expected to be "artisans or masters of their crafts."

ABET's clear conception of what constitutes a collegiate education distinguishes it from many other specialized bodies accrediting at the two-year level. It is noteworthy that more attention is devoted to communications education in ABET (n.d.) than to any other curriculum element, technical specialties included. The ABET rationale for the study of communications is quoted here to illustrate how an accreditation body can conceive of general education in terms of the liberal dimension that it adds to professional competence and, as a consequence, take responsibility for ensuring its reinforcement within the curriculum: "Good oral and written communications are considered by ABET to be a necessary achievement of a college graduate. Technically trained individuals should not be considered educated regardless of the depth of their technical capability if they cannot communicate, both orally and in writing, their technical findings, thoughts, and philosophy to others around them. . . . It must be evident to the visiting team that graduates are proficient in the use of the English language and have developed the ability to communicate ideas and understand those of others" (n.d., p. 7).

American Assembly of Collegiate Schools of Business (AACSB). AACSB accredits only baccalaureate and master's degree programs. In a frequently reaffirmed statement (AACSB, 1987), however, it acknowledges that its accreditation criteria do influence two- to four-year college program articulation and student transfer. Among the accreditation bodies examined here, AACSB is the only one to explicitly encourage four-year institutions to enter into regional articulation agreements that assign transfer parity for courses at the respective institutions to obviate transfer difficulties to the greatest extent possible. At the same time, it is the only specialized accreditation body whose transfer stance has aroused the ire and political energies of the community college movement at local, state, and national levels (for a convenient summary of the debate, see Robertson-Smith, 1988).

The offending principle is AACSB's (n.d., p. 22) declaration that "whether or not an articulation agreement is present, the baccalaureate degree-granting institution will use validation procedures each time a student takes a course at the lower-division level which the degree-granting institution offers at the upper-division level and which is to be accepted for upper-division credit in business administration or economics." AACSB urges that this policy be read in the context of its call for a broad undergraduate curriculum responsive to social, economic, and technological change, both domestic and global. Consequently, it stipulates that the first two years of undergraduate education, wherever located, provide what it calls "descriptive and analytical" (n.d., p. 28) foundations for business studies by emphasizing liberal arts and sciences and by limiting professional courses to introductory offerings. Critics maintain that AACSB's standards at best ignore distinctive differences of institutional mission and at worst subvert the distinctive educational needs of community college clientele.

In one sense, AACSB has enriched substantially the discussion about transfer readiness of community college students by reasserting a principle of university parallelism for two-year college studies. In another sense, it has exacerbated the dilemma of access. Community colleges enroll a preponderance of working adults and minority students whose attraction to career-oriented business curricula is by necessity often motivated by short-term occupational outcomes. When these students decide later to pursue baccalaureate degrees, they face credit loss for coursework according to a logic asserting that courses taken as freshmen and sophomores may not count toward the baccalaureate degree, even if required in that curriculum, because they were taken at the "wrong level" as defined by an accreditation body (one that does not even admit community colleges to its membership).

Policies and Practices: Regional Agencies

Any system of voluntary accreditation must inevitably balance agency prescription against institutional autonomy. Put another way, any philosophy of accreditation, as currently conceived, is tempered by its politics. And much of the current debate about strengthening accreditation has been focused on how to preserve that balance while providing genuine assurances to the larger community that academic programs have been rigorously conceived, delivered, and evaluated (Davies, 1987). In the language of the Commission on Higher Education (1982, p. 1), "Accreditation is the educational community's means of self-regulation. The accrediting process is intended to strengthen and sustain the quality and integrity of higher education, making it worthy of public confidence and minimizing the scope and exercise of government control."

In maintaining the principle of self-regulation, however, the regional associations have tended to ignore issues of transfer and articulation, issues that are inextricably linked to issues of equity and access, thereby inviting the intervention of extramural bodies such as foundations and quasi-governmental and governmental agencies. On the whole, the regional agencies have also ignored state and national endorsements of stronger liberal arts and science requirements for the associate degree. For a number of years, for example, the state of New Jersey has required a minimum of twenty and thirty general education credits for the associate degrees in applied science and science, respectively. It now requires that all associate degree curricula select from an array of general education courses, with at least one course each from the categories of communications, mathematics and science, social science, and humanities (State of New Jersey, 1986). The American Association of Community and Junior Colleges (1989) adopted a nonbinding but consensus-driven policy statement in 1984 calling for varying thresholds of general education for associate degrees in arts, science, and applied science, and its affiliate National Council for Occupational Education (1985) adopted related criteria, supporting the concept of a liberally educated community college technical graduate.

Although the Commission on Colleges of the Southern Association of Colleges and Schools has adopted criteria requiring a minimum of fifteen hours of general education in two-year programs, the regional accreditors, on the whole, still eschew definition of even base-line standards for general education curricula, for faculty preparation in occupational curricula, and for transfer and articulation efforts. The Middle States Association, for example, stipulates that "professional usefulness should not be the only ground on which courses are selected and general education components should not be limited to courses which develop communication and computation skills" (Commission on Higher Education, 1982, p. 9), leaving the decision entirely to the institutions or, by default, to the states to determine the nature, content, and extent of general education in the curriculum. While there is much in the guidelines' language that encourages institutional efforts, there is little that sets benchmarks for internal or external judgments about whether or not an institution is cultivating the communications and analytical skills, as well as humanistic and social perspectives, that make possible an intellectual and scholarly continuity between the associate and the baccalaureate degrees.

As currently conceived, the emphasis placed on institutional self-assessment by most regional accreditation bodies need not exclude, but does not specifically include, attention to areas that require interinstitutional coordination, such as transfer and articulation. That is, there is typically no specific mandate in the regional review process for a college or university to take into account the goals set by other local or feeder institutions and the ensuing need for a collaborative response. The Middle States Association's *Characteristics of Excellence,* for example, refers to transfer only in passing, and then merely as an aspect of a college's placement and counseling function in relation to students who encounter "special problems" in their attempts to transfer (Commission on Higher Education, 1982, p. 15).

Accreditation Agencies' Potential to Mitigate Elitism

As documented by Kells and Parrish (1986), the specialized accreditation of career-oriented programs at two-year, regionally accredited colleges contributed substantially to the overall growth in accreditation activity between 1978 and 1985. By 1980, the Council on Postsecondary Education (COPA) had already recognized thirty-nine specialized accreditation or approval bodies, one of which, CAHEA, sponsors eighteen different allied health review committees. The number of these bodies may well increase given emerging specializations and the status that the authority to certify programs appears to convey. In more recent years, COPA has responded to at least seventy-two inquiries from groups interested in establishing accreditation procedures (Glidden, 1983). In addition to the five accreditation agencies reviewed above, there are a host of others with direct authority over associate degree programs—among them, the National Association of Schools of Art and Design, the American Dental Association, the American Dietetic Association, the American Bar Association, the American Physical Therapy Association, and the CAHEA-allied health review committees. There are also agencies that do not accredit two-year programs but whose standards bear on two-year curricula in terms of lower- and upper-level program correspondences and transference, such as the Society of American Foresters, the American Council on Construction Education, and the Council on Social Work Education.

Accreditation and General Education. The proliferation of specialized accreditation agencies and their activities is the most commonly voiced complaint by institutional leaders about accreditation, for a variety of reasons ranging from costs to the institution to usurpation of campus prerogatives in determining program standards (Glidden, 1983; Kells and Parrish, 1986). In a 1986 American Council on Education (ACE) survey of accreditation issues, only 65 percent of two-year college chief executive officers and other officials believed that "specialized accreditation assures me that the standards and quality of my programs are generally acceptable in the postsecondary education community" (Anderson, 1987, p. 7), compared to 81 percent of university and 73 percent of comprehensive and baccalaureate institutions, respectively. Forty-nine percent of all respondents believed that "course requirements make it difficult for the institution to achieve the breadth of knowledge it wants its graduates to have" (Anderson, 1987, p. 7). Of the twenty-four questions asked about specialized accreditation activity, those pertaining to general education aroused the most negative responses. Of the 374 respondents, 61 percent (73 percent at baccalaureate and 56 percent at associate degree institutions) faulted the accreditation process because it limited the amount of general education that students could take. A COPA (1986, p. 2) advisory panel validated, as the first of four general criticisms of the accreditation enterprise, that "too often accreditation is based on minimal statistical standards without an insistence on higher quality in the process of teaching and learning and general education."

Accreditation and Faculty Qualifications. Neither the ACE (Anderson, 1987) nor the COPA (1986) study addresses the issue of faculty qualifications in occupational-technical curricula. Some of the program directors in the five accredited disciplines reviewed above had academic credentials superior to those required by the respective approval bodies. Many had less. Only NLN requires the master's as the minimum degree for community college specialty course teaching; ABET requires only that the majority of faculty have master's degrees or be professionally certified; and NAACLS and JRCERT, in the allied health fields, require no degree higher than the baccalaureate, if that. Yet, it is reasonable to assume a correlation between a faculty's own educational attainment and its grasp of the contextual and communications competencies needed to help career students locate their technical study within larger historical, social, economic, scientific, and political realities. It is also reasonable to assume a correlation between the professoriate's concern for its own scholarly improvement and the imperative that is felt to motivate career-oriented students to seek professional mobility or personal growth through persistence beyond the associate degree.

Accreditation and Access. Both two- and four-year colleges have a stake in realizing student transfer from vocational and nonvocational curricula into baccalaureate degree programs. For the community colleges, transfer confirms a collegiate identity within the higher education community while fulfilling a goal to provide access to four-year degrees for those who otherwise might not have such access. All sectors of higher education have a vested self-interest as well as a social interest in promoting the education of minority and working-class students. Ironically, the AACSB leadership recently warned its members that graduate business schools risk a serious overall decline in enrollment if the numbers of black and Hispanic students continue to decrease (French, 1987). Should minority students presently enrolled in community college career-oriented business programs eventually seek baccalaureate or master's degrees, they may be prevented from transferring all of their credits. If for no better reason than enrollment management, senior colleges and universities should see the long-term, enlightened self-interest in their connections to community college programs and students and reconsider their transfer postures accordingly.

Although the substance of AACSB's current standoff with the community colleges is principled, the focus of the confrontation on access is helping to obscure significant issues related to programmatic articulation and student transfer, such as the validity of academic parallelism and of a liberal arts and science foundation in the first two years of all undergraduate curricula. These issues should be debated within higher education by all accreditation bodies and their constituencies in the quest for improved transfer education.

Accreditation and Articulation. Because they review individual institutions and individual institutional programs, accreditation agencies, regional and specialized, generally have not made intersector and interinstitutional student and programmatic articulation a priority. This is especially true of medical auxiliary education programs such as respiratory therapy, radiation therapy, and medical laboratory science where there is no well-defined associate to baccalaureate degree sequence.

Toward an Agenda

After years of attempts by many colleges and universities to resolve substantive differences, including the disenfranchisement of the two-year sector, the recent creation of the Association of Collegiate Business Schools and Programs has effectively ended AACSB's seventy-year reign. Most of us would probably agree that resolution of differences through the creation of alternative agencies represents an extreme that threatens to undermine the special interrelationships between institutions of higher education and the accreditation community. At the same time, the formation of the new association illustrates the strength of a uniquely American system of academic governance by pointing to the ability and the will of higher education institutions to bring about change from within. Short of duplicating accreditation bodies within disciplines, however, how can faculty and administrators use that strength to promote transfer-enhancing policies in accreditation organizations?

Setting the Agenda. First and foremost, faculty and administrators can set the agenda by making the topic of accreditation and its relationship to two- and four-year program articulation a matter of broader concern: research it, write about it, and address it in public forums. Very little, for example, has been written about the congruence of general education reform and accreditation standards. Still less has been noted about the logistics of student transfer to baccalaureate degree programs in the light of diverse professional association criteria for two- and four-year programs.

Moving the Agenda. Next, we need to move the agenda by engaging the accreditation community in a dialogue about the effects of their policies on transfer. It is not nurse practitioners alone, for example, who should be deciding whether or not there shall be career ladder continuity between associate and baccalaureate degree nurses. Assurance of educational and occupational mobility to two-year program students fulfills a larger social mission that makes programmatic articulation an important issue for all of us. It is, therefore, critical that individuals and higher educational constituencies demonstrate greater interest in selecting those who represent them within accreditation bodies, better acquaint themselves with the issues confronting associations, and seek dialogue with the associations about transfer education.

Minimally, at the national level, we should call upon COPA, the national umbrella organization of accreditation agencies, to study the transfer-enabling guidelines (or their absence) of constituent members. This study should be sought with a view toward requesting COPA advocacy of policies that promote student transfer and program articulation between two- and four-year colleges. And, at the state level, we should insist that those with oversight or regulatory authority exert more substantive influence on regional and specialized accreditation reviews of state-supported institutions of higher education, especially in cases where those reviews are accepted for licensure in lieu of state evaluations. At a minimum, state higher education officers should be asked to promote policies requiring, wherever possible during the accreditation process, that four-year institutions document efforts to encourage student transfer from and program articulation with two-year campuses.

Accreditation and Transfer. In the current transfer context, community and other two-year colleges need support. Most four-year institutions have little incentive to work with their two-year counterparts in reducing transfer barriers. If the policies and practices of the agencies reviewed above are accurate indicators, then it is apparent that accreditation bodies, regional and specialized, do not yet envision themselves as agents of change promoting the conditions necessary to facilitate transfer from two- to four-year institutions. If we are to improve student and institutional transfer relationships from within higher education, and if we are to reach consensus on transfer-related issues such as programmatic and student articulation, we must provide direction to accreditation bodies about underlying structural factors such as curriculum parallelism and delivery, career program faculty qualifications, and interinstitutional relationships.

References

Accreditation Board for Engineering and Technology. *Criteria for Accrediting Programs in Engineering Technology: Effective for Evaluations During the 1987–88 Academic Year.* New York: Accreditation Board for Engineering and Technology, n.d.

American Assembly of Collegiate Schools of Business. *Accreditation Council Policies, Procedures, and Standards (1987–88).* St. Louis, Mo.: American Assembly of Collegiate Schools of Business, n.d.

American Assembly of Collegiate Schools of Business. *Statement of the Standards Committee on Those Accreditation Council Standards Bearing on Junior and Community College Relations.* St. Louis, Mo.: American Assembly of Collegiate Schools of Business, 1987.

American Association of Community and Junior Colleges. *Policy Statements of the American Association of Community and Junior Colleges.* Washington, D.C.: American Association of Community and Junior Colleges, 1989. 32 pp. (ED 311 997)

Anderson, C. *Survey of Higher Accreditation Issues, 1986.* Higher Education Panel Reports, no. 74. Washington, D.C.: American Council on Education, 1987. 47 pp. (ED 283 427)

Bader-Borel, P. (ed.). *Compilation of Statistical Data Concerning the Community Colleges of the State University of New York, 1983–84.* Albany: Office for Community Colleges, State University of New York, 1984. 368 pp. (ED 253 280)

Baron, R. F. "The Change from Transfer to Career Education at Community Colleges in the 1970s." *Community/Junior College Quarterly of Research and Practice,* 1982, 7 (1), 71–87.

Bernstein, A. "The Devaluation of Transfer: Current Explanations and Possible Causes." In L. S. Zwerling (ed.), *The Community College and Its Critics.* New Directions for Community Colleges, no. 54. San Francisco: Jossey-Bass, 1986.

Cohen, A. M. *Counting the Transfer Students.* Junior College Resource Review. Los Angeles: ERIC Clearinghouse for Junior Colleges, 1979. 6 pp. (ED 172 864)

Cohen, A. M., and Brawer, F. B. *The American Community College.* (2nd ed.) San Francisco: Jossey-Bass, 1989.

Commission on Higher Education. *Characteristics of Excellence: Standards for Accreditation.* Philadelphia: Middle States Association of Schools and Colleges, 1982.

Council on Postsecondary Accreditation. *COPA Self-Study Advisory Panel. Findings and Recommendations Submitted to the Board of Directors, the Council on Postsecondary Accreditation.* Washington, D.C.: Council on Postsecondary Accreditation, 1986. 51 pp. (ED 197 683)

Davies, G. K. "Accreditation and Society." *North Central Accreditation Quarterly,* 1987, *62* (2), 380-385.

French, H. W. "Business Schools Warned on Decline of Minorities." *New York Times,* Dec. 13, 1987, p. 135.

Glidden, R. "Specialized Accreditation." In K. E. Young, C. M. Chambers, H. R. Kells, and Associates. *Understanding Accreditation: Contemporary Perspectives on Issues and Practices in Evaluating Educational Quality.* San Francisco: Jossey-Bass, 1983.

Hunter, R., and Sheldon, M. S. *Statewide Longitudinal Study: Report on Academic Year, 1979–80. Part 3: Fall Results.* Woodland Hills, Calif.: Los Angeles Pierce College, 1980. 95 pp. (ED 188 714)

Joint Review Committee on Education in Radiologic Technology. *Essentials and Guidelines of an Accredited Education Program for the Radiation Therapy Technologist.* N.p.: Joint Review Committee on Education in Radiologic Technology, 1981.

Joint Review Committee on Education in Radiologic Technology. *Essentials and Guidelines of an Accredited Education Program for the Radiographer.* N.p.: Joint Review Committee on Education in Radiologic Technology, 1983.

Karabel, J. "Community Colleges and Social Stratification." In L. S. Zwerling (ed.), *The Community College and Its Critics.* New Directions for Community Colleges, no. 54. San Francisco: Jossey-Bass, 1986.

Kells, H. R., and Parrish, R. M. *Trends in the Accreditation Relationships of U.S. Postsecondary Institutions, 1978–1985.* Washington, D.C.: Council on Postsecondary Accreditation, 1986. 17 pp. (ED 297 684)

Kissler, G. R. "The Decline of the Transfer Function: Threats or Challenges?" In F. C. Kintzer (ed.), *Improving Articulation and Transfer Relationships.* New Directions for Community Colleges, no. 39. San Francisco: Jossey-Bass, 1982.

Knoell, D. "The Transfer Function—One of Many." In F. C. Kintzer (ed.), *Improving Articulation and Transfer Relationships.* New Directions for Community Colleges, no. 39. San Francisco: Jossey-Bass, 1982.

Lombardi, J. *The Decline of Transfer Education.* Topical Papers, no. 70. Los Angeles: ERIC Clearinghouse for Junior Colleges, 1979. 37 pp. (ED 179 273)

National Accrediting Agency for Clinical Laboratory Sciences. *Essentials and Guidelines of Accredited Educational Programs for the Medical Laboratory Technician.* N.p.: National Accrediting Agency for Clinical Laboratory Sciences, 1986.

National Council for Occupational Education. *Criteria for Excellence in Associate in Applied Science Degree Programs.* National Council for Occupational Education Monograph Series, vol. 2, no. 1. Washington, D.C.: National Council for Occupational Education and American Association of Community and Junior Colleges, 1985. 12 pp. (ED 278 430)

National League for Nursing. *Criteria for the Evaluation of Associate Degree Programs in Nursing.* New York: National League for Nursing, 1982a.

National League for Nursing. *Position Statement on Educational Mobility.* New York: National League for Nursing, 1982b.

Oromaner, M. "Insiders, Outsiders, and the Community College: A Sociology of Knowledge Perspective." *Research in Higher Education,* 1984, *21* (2), 226-235.

Palmer, J. "Bolstering the Community College Transfer Function: An ERIC Review." *Community College Review,* 1987, *14* (3), 53-63.

Pincus, L. "Vocational Education: More False Promises." In L. S. Zwerling (ed.), *The Community College and Its Critics.* New Directions for Community Colleges, no. 54. San Francisco: Jossey-Bass, 1986.

Prager, C. "The Other Transfer Degree." In C. Prager (ed.), *Enhancing Articulation and Transfer.* New Directions for Community Colleges, no. 61. San Francisco: Jossey-Bass, 1988.

Robertson-Smith, M. "Specialized Accreditation and Articulation of Business Programs." In C. Prager (ed.), *Enhancing Articulation and Transfer.* New Directions for Community Colleges, no. 61. San Francisco: Jossey-Bass, 1988.

State of New Jersey. *Regulations and Standards for the New Jersey Community Colleges.* Trenton, N.J.: Department of Higher Education, 1986.

CAROLYN PRAGER is former vice president of academic affairs at Hudson County Community College, Jersey City, New Jersey, and former state director of community colleges for New Jersey. She is currently chief executive officer of the Community Campus of The Pennsylvania State University, University Park.

Community colleges have worked and are working with universities and four-year colleges in a variety of consortia; these partnerships have enhanced and will continue to enhance the stature of community colleges in the United States.

Gaining Stature Through Community College-University Consortia

Gwen May, Al Smith

The role of the community college is to help prepare all citizens of its community for a better life. In a rapidly changing society, the responsibilities to educate and prepare these people to live and function in an information age define a difficult task. In order to meet the demands placed on them, community colleges need to stay abreast of the advances made in technology and of the changing needs of society. An increasing number of jobs now require an education beyond high school, and many people are returning to school to be retrained for jobs that did not exist several years ago. More minority and disadvantaged students, who previously might not have attended college, are also entering community colleges. As the number of typical college-age students dwindles and our population ages, community colleges will see fewer and fewer students who fit the traditional college student profile.

The task of preparing students to work in a technological society is expensive, and funding has not kept up with the needs. State governments and government agencies are expecting more of postsecondary education institutions as they implement legislation to improve overall education in the United States. Community colleges have a significant role to play in this improvement effort and will face many challenges in the years ahead. How well those challenges are met will affect the stature of community colleges and the country's ability to compete in the world.

When groups or individuals want to achieve a goal, they often band together in order to strengthen their position and increase their chances of achieving that goal. Consortia of community colleges and universities appear to be one of the best vehicles that community colleges can use to meet the challenges placed before them and to establish and maintain their proper place in the educational community. In this chapter, we look at the history of these consortia, the problems facing community colleges, and some of the cooperative endeavors already underway that show how consortia can be instrumental in raising community and national awareness of the importance of community colleges in the educational structure of our society.

History of Consortia

Cooperation between colleges and universities began on an informal level as early as the nineteenth century. As the organization and administration of programs became more complex, the need for more formal systems began to develop in the 1950s. During the 1960s, a great increase in the number of students attending postsecondary institutions brought many new problems. Because of expanding curricula and the increasing number of new courses offered, colleges and universities needed more qualified and diverse faculty, more money to teach expensive courses requiring costly technology, and more funding for research.

Higher education looked to institutional cooperation as a way to help solve some of these problems. Cooperative programs developed rapidly, and institutions devised similar academic calendars, created joint departments, shared faculty expertise and specialized facilities, and together obtained grants.

The purpose and membership of consortia vary a great deal. Although the broad goal of every consortium is to "achieve more, do something better, or reduce the cost of an activity" (Neal, 1988, p. 3), each consortium is unique. A consortium's purpose may require members to be located in close proximity, while another consortium may allow institutions to be as geographically separated as the East and West coasts. There is no formula for a successful consortium, but earlier endeavors indicate several key ingredients in those that continue to produce effective results. A strong consortium needs to have specific, well-defined goals, strong support from high-level administrators in each of the member institutions, adequate funding, and an organization director who stimulates and communicates effectively with each institution.

Based on their own records of achievement, it is clear that community college consortia can raise awareness about community colleges and produce effective results. In 1968, the League for Innovation in the Community College was founded by B. Lamar Johnson. Since that time, "the League has sponsored eighty-two conferences, sixty-nine publications, ten special projects, and sixty-eight projects funded for $24,136,296" (O'Banion, 1988, p. 46). The League for Innovation in the Community College has given community colleges opportunities to share information and participate in activities such as innovative programs, leadership development, and summer seminars abroad. Fryer (1986, p. 21) notes that consortia are a cost-effective way to work on problems faced by community colleges: "In Northern California the Learning Assessment and Retention Consortium . . . has probably done more to improve educational practice in the areas of basic skills assessment and retention than laws, regulations, or a dozen state chancellor's office task forces could."

Community Colleges in the 1990s

As institutions look at the problems facing them, and their available options, they have turned again in the 1990s, as they did in the 1960s and 1970s, to interinstitutional cooperation. The problems that community colleges are facing today—declining enrollments, nontraditional students, rapidly expanding needs for information and technology, and declines in funding—are different from those of two decades ago, but they are equally as serious. Community colleges are more likely to successfully address the challenges through cooperative efforts rather than in isolation.

The ideas expressed by Patterson and Ackley in 1979 seem to hold true today. They stated that colleges and universities in the 1980s and early 1990s would be faced with four alternatives when confronting the issues of a changing student population and a reduction in funding: "Survive alone, develop substantial voluntary cooperation, accept publicly mandated coordination, or terminate operation" (Patterson and Ackley, 1979, p. 1). It seems unlikely that any institution would willingly choose to terminate operation. It also seems unlikely that an institution would be willing to relinquish its authority to publicly mandated coordination. Thus, only two alternatives are left. Some large institutions, with equally large endowments and/or high tuition, could probably survive in isolation without affecting the quality of education provided. But community colleges do not fit into this category. Community colleges would have a difficult time continuing to serve their constituencies adequately without sacrificing programs, quality, and services. Therefore, it seems a logical choice for community colleges to look toward interinstitutional cooperation as a way to meet the demands of the 1990s. Through consortia, community colleges can continue to provide leadership, establish new programs, and provide new services to their communities. In this way, they will be able to maintain and continue to strengthen their place in the educational community.

The biggest and most often cited advantage of interinstitutional membership is that cooperation helps end the isolation found in higher education. Not only does a consortium enhance communication between institutions, but it also seems to enhance communication on individual campuses by giving administrators, faculty, staff, and students a greater opportunity to share interests and ideas. Consortia can help higher education institutions increase their contribution to their communities, help small colleges survive, and minimize the need for formal legislative action. Interinstitutional cooperation can allow colleges and universities to expand research programs to include more individual research and to explore in more depth specific areas of need, especially as they relate to teaching and learning.

In a rapidly changing world, there are many areas where cooperative efforts can be beneficial to institutions and to prospective students, especially in the areas of computers and related technologies: "The new technologies have shifted the importance of the written word in favor of sound and images. Research is done differently. Retraining is as important as preparation for a career in the first place. Most workers will depend on computers in some way or other within a very few years. Large data bases make information readily available. The personal nature of the technologies has put the learner in charge" (Strange, 1988, pp. 165–166).

A close look at five consortia reveals how cooperative efforts have enabled each of them to achieve goals and have increased the educational stature of the community colleges as they work together to provide services and increase institutional effectiveness.

Central Florida Consortium of Higher Education

The Central Florida Consortium of Higher Education was conceived by university administrators who wanted to share resources with nearby community colleges. In 1988, the University of Central Florida and Valencia Community College began discussions. Soon after, Seminole Community College joined them to begin forming the consortium. By fall 1988, three other community colleges indicated their interest in the organization. In early 1989, the Central Florida Consortium of Higher Education was formally established (E. Greenwood, personal communication, April 18, 1983).

The consortium is composed of Brevard Community College, Daytona Beach Community College, Lake-Sumter Community College, Seminole Community College, Valencia Community College, and the University of Central Florida. All of these community colleges are within close proximity of the university. Most of the students who transfer to four-year institutions from these community colleges choose the University of Central Florida. A high percentage of the University of Central Florida's undergraduate student body has attended a nearby community college. These institutions saw that by working together they could enhance the educational opportunities of students in the area. The consortium's purpose, then, was to coordinate activities that focused on common goals and concerns.

The first consortium-sponsored activity was a one-day general education workshop held in February 1989. This workshop addressed state mandates about testing, writing, and foreign language instruction. Discipline-specific work sessions allowed faculty from the different institutions to discuss general education requirements and common issues in the respective disciplines. The workshop gave faculty and administrators an opportunity to learn about other institutions in their area and to begin to develop networks for solving common problems. As a result of this general education workshop, the mathematics faculties of these institutions decided to meet on a regular basis to discuss and better coordinate the integration of new technologies into their courses.

The next workshop came only a month later. This day was devoted to topics on leadership and administrative skills in an academic environment. So successful was this workshop that the following year a series of four leadership workshops were scheduled, focusing on such topics as team building, conflict resolution, increases in productivity, and performance appraisal.

Although the Central Florida Consortium of Higher Education is a relatively young organization, it has many projects underway and many others in beginning stages. With one member institution taking the lead, the consortium cosponsored a workshop on the issues associated with increased use of adjunct faculty. The workshop sessions gave supervisors of adjunct faculty the opportunity to discuss the efficiency of current institutional policies and procedures, personnel and legal issues, orientation, and faculty development. A workshop for registrars and admission, records, and financial aid officers forged new articulation efforts to smooth the transfer process for community college graduates moving on to the university.

Other projects include a conference on institutional effectiveness, graduate courses in various disciplines provided by university faculty for community college faculty, and a weeklong writing-across-the-curriculum workshop for faculty in disciplines other than English who want to integrate writing and critical thinking skills more fully into their curricula.

Elaine Greenwood, executive director of the Central Florida Consortium of Higher Education, has observed that subtle changes take place when community colleges and universities work together. The benefits of their workshops and cooperative efforts have been obvious, but she has seen changes in the perceptions of the community college both from the university and the community. A mutual respect has developed among colleagues as a result of their work together. The community colleges and the consortium now receive more publicity and recognition from the media. For the Central Florida Consortium of Higher Education as a whole and the community colleges that are members, recognition and respect have come quickly. As this consortium further develops, the community colleges will continue to see their stature in the educational community grow.

Community College Consortium:
University of Michigan, Michigan State University,
and University of Toledo

In 1986, the University of Michigan met with eight regional community college presidents to learn about the needs of their institutions. As an outgrowth of that meeting, the Community College Consortium was established in 1987 with the University of Michigan and forty-five community colleges from across the country. Within a year, the University of Toledo joined the consortium as a sponsoring institution. Soon after, Michigan State University became the consortium's third sponsor. Presently, the consortium has a membership of seventy-five community colleges located in eighteen states and Canada. Approximately two-thirds of the membership come from the states of Indiana, Illinois, Ohio, Kansas, Missouri, Iowa, Nebraska, Michigan, Wisconsin, Minnesota, North Dakota, and South Dakota.

The overarching theme of the Community College Consortium is improvement of institutional effectiveness in the primary areas of leadership, strategic management, and teaching and learning. The consortium sponsors four professional development institutes each year. The Community College Summer Institute, held in June, focuses on institutional effectiveness and student success. This institute addresses institutional effectiveness in practical terms, looks at recent research, and presents exemplary programs. The Faculty Professional Development Institute, held in November, is designed specifically for new faculty. This institute addresses factors that influence and affect community colleges, examines problems and issues that relate to teaching and learning, and provides techniques and ideas that improve learning. In February, the Emerging Leaders Institute is held for educational personnel who have been identified as emerging leaders at their institutions. The purpose of this institute is to discuss the evolving mission of community colleges, the challenges facing leaders, decision making, and strategic management using the technique of case study analysis. The Strategic Leadership Institute, held in May or June, is for community college executive officers. The focus of this institute is on issues facing community colleges and on long-range planning.

The Community College Consortium also conducts one research project each year. The most recent project examines how institutional effectiveness is viewed at community colleges. Four times each year the consortium also publishes a newsletter for its members. This newsletter addresses current issues facing community colleges, gives information regarding coming events, and includes articles of interest to faculty, staff, and administrators. Each year the consortium sponsors a reception for its members at the national convention of the American Association of Community and Junior Colleges.

Richard Alfred, one of the codirectors of the consortium, believes that the consortium has helped community colleges build stature in the educational community by strengthening and building the units within the organization. He believes that the Emerging Leaders Institute has broadened the management skills of community college leaders and thus has helped develop better executive officers for community colleges. The institute for new and recently appointed faculty has helped prepare these faculty for the reality of the classroom. They learn from experienced community college instructors, not only about teaching and learning techniques but also about the mission and philosophy of community colleges. Through research, the consortium has helped build theories and knowledge that support the role of community colleges. When community college leaders view their institutions as public service organizations, they can do a better job of presenting their institution to the public. Like most people who are involved with institutional cooperation, Alfred points out that the consortium facilitates networking among the member institutions. In this way, they can help and learn from one another (R. Alfred, personal communication, August 10, 1989).

As community colleges continue to strengthen their leadership, develop their personnel, and address the changes that face their institutions, they become models in the educational community. This consortium began with one university sponsor and within a short time there were three other universities involved. Through this cosponsorship and the mutual interests and benefits, these community colleges and universities are working together. The Community College Consortium demonstrates how community colleges are enhancing their image and increasing their stature in the educational community.

Florida Community Junior College Inter-Institutional Research Council

The Florida Community Junior College Inter-Institutional Research Council (IRC) is a consortium designed to encourage and promote research in community colleges. When IRC formally began in 1969, its membership included the University of Florida and fifteen of the state's community colleges. Membership in the consortium is open to all community colleges in Florida, and the number of community colleges participating in the organization varies from year to year (J. Wattenbarger, personal communication, September 5, 1989).

The consortium was established on the belief that it could offer research opportunities to member community colleges that would otherwise not be available to individual institutions working alone. Research is costly and time-consuming, which often precludes its pursuit at the community college level. By working cooperatively, the institutions in this consortium share in the cost of research and each member has access to the results. The University of Florida provides consultants and advisers in such areas as research design, data analysis, and publication.

The goals of IRC are to provide information that can be used to improve learning, increase institutional effectiveness, and examine and improve educational programs. One of IRC's original goals also included making contributions in the area of institutional management and organization by providing research models to members and other postsecondary institutions.

Research conducted by individual colleges tends to have a narrow focus and a limited range of applicability and is therefore rarely useful to other institutions. The opportunity to publish the results of this research and receive recognition for the effort is often limited. When research involves a group of community colleges, however, the opportunity to publish is greatly enhanced because the results can be generalized to institutions beyond those studied. IRC has published many articles in professional journals and, as a result, has brought stature to the consortium and the member community colleges.

In 1979, after ten years of operation, IRC conducted a self-study in order to look at its strengths and weaknesses. Through this research, the consortium gained information about its past projects that helped it focus on the goals of the next decade. During those next ten years, IRC continued to carry out pilot studies, provide in-service development activities for its members, maintain a list of research projects, and provide resources and consultants to its member institutions. IRC continues to provide these institutions with a valuable communications link and an avenue for continued improvement of community colleges in Florida through research.

The sheer quantity of publications and journal articles that were produced as a result of this interinstitutional cooperation demonstrates that IRC has contributed substantially to the stature of community colleges. With the recognition by many in higher education, from regional boards to state departments of public education, of the work done by this consortium and its member community colleges, it is clear that the community college is establishing itself in the educational community.

Michigan Colleges' Consortium for Faculty Development

Currently, the membership of the Michigan Colleges' Consortium for Faculty Development is composed of five community colleges and one university. Macomb Community College, Monroe County Community College, Oakland Community College, Schoolcraft College, Washtenaw Community College, and the University of Michigan at Dearborn work together to produce teaching modules for faculty development. The community colleges select the subject for each of the teaching modules and then work as advisers with the University of Michigan at Dearborn to produce high-quality videotapes and manuals.

This self-supporting consortium began in 1983 as an informal task force. The School of Education and Professional and Adult Continuing Education at the University of Michigan at Dearborn was interested in working with community colleges to help them prepare their part-time faculty for the classroom. The community colleges saw this offer as an opportunity to continue to increase the quality of instruction at their institutions. Eight local community colleges were contacted about the proposal, and, as a result, Monroe County Community College, Oakland Community College, and Schoolcraft College met with university representatives to make suggestions for potential workshops to be conducted by the university. This task force continued to meet and, over the next year, identified and designed the format for the workshop modules. During fall 1985, the first series of manuals and videotapes were developed: *Course Goals and Objectives, The First Day, Planning the Lesson,* and *Planning Instruction for Higher Levels of Thought.*

One factor contributing to the growth and success of these workshops was that the participating institutions viewed these first sessions as a beginning, a pilot. For this reason, those involved took more risks because they knew that they were not delivering a final product. When faculty members from the University of Michigan at Dearborn conducted the original workshops at the participating community colleges, they knew that there would be changes to make in the videotapes and manuals. The institutions were working together to produce a good product. Openness and communication between institutions were important ingredients in making this a successful project.

As expected, the task force made adjustments in its original plans after the first workshops were completed. One of the first changes was the expansion of the target audience to include new full-time faculty as well as the original audience of part-time faculty. In order to raise money to produce additional modules, the task force also decided to market these faculty development modules to other community colleges and universities. At that time, it was also decided to make the modules self-contained. The videotapes and manuals would be designed so that they could be used by facilitators at any institution.

After approximately three years, in 1986, the task force established itself as a consortium, and its activities underwent rapid change during the next few years. Major revisions were made in the first two modules, and the consortium began focusing more of its efforts on marketing the new modules. By early 1987, revision of the second two modules was completed. Also, the consortium doubled its community college membership when Macomb Community College, Mott Community College, and Washtenaw Community College joined the organization. Teaching modules on cross-cultural communication and assessment of evaluation methods were developed during 1987. In 1988, the consortium achieved another goal when it became self-supporting.

By 1989, the consortium members agreed to develop at least one new teaching module each year. The existing modules would continue to be reevaluated and updated. The consortium coordinator continues to play a major role in the success of the consortium by gaining increased exposure for the College Teaching Faculty Development Series modules. The videotapes and manuals have been exhibited at such conferences as the American Association of Community and Junior Colleges and the American Association of Higher Education. Advertisements for this series have also appeared in the *Chronicle of Higher Education* and *T.H.E. Journal*. The consortium sponsored its first conference on faculty instructional development in 1990.

Mary Minter, the consortium coordinator, has witnessed how the consortium approach has brought recognition and stature to its member community colleges. Moreover, within each individual community college there is a sense of prestige connected to the involvement of the faculty in consortium development activities, and across member institutions there is a feeling of leadership and pride in being associated with a project that has become financially self-supporting and successful (including support for a full-time coordinator). The participating community colleges have gained recognition throughout the entire educational community as other institutions learn about the teaching modules and look to the consortium as a source of and guide to more effective college teaching (M. Minter, personal communication, July 26, 1989).

North Texas Community/Junior College Consortium

In February 1989, the University of North Texas (UNT) invited community and junior colleges in the north Texas area to a meeting to discuss the establishment of a consortium for community colleges. By July 1989, nine community and junior college districts and fifteen colleges had indicated their interest in becoming involved in cooperative efforts with UNT and community colleges in the area. Collin County Community College District, Cooke County College, Dallas County Community College District, Grayson County College, Kilgore College, Navarro College, Paris Junior College, Trinity Valley Community College, and Weatherford College comprise the college districts that now work together on research and professional development activities for the improvement of community college education in north Texas.

The North Texas Community/Junior College Consortium (NTC/JCC) is currently organizing conferences and workshops on two topics: research in developmental education and in faculty development. Research in developmental education will provide the participating colleges with procedures for establishing and improving developmental education programs that produce accountable results. Consortium members hope that this research also will result in more funding from the state for state-mandated developmental programs. The faculty development conferences and workshops will emphasize networking among faculty in the consortium, faculty discussion of methods to increase student success and of innovative teaching techniques, and new opportunities for professional growth. For example, the fall 1991 conference, Issues of the Nineties: Quality, Access, Diversity, Leadership, and Management, included an academic advising seminar, field trips to innovative facilities, presentations of research findings, program descriptions, demonstrations, workshops on teaching techniques, and papers addressing each of the targeted issues.

One of the authors of this chapter, Al Smith, was formerly executive director of NTC/JCC. He believes that this new and growing partnership will bring additional stature and recognition to the community colleges in north Texas. He thinks that regional university-community college partnerships are a wave of the future and predicts that the number of regional, two-year and four-year college consortia will expand rapidly over the next ten years as universities and four-year colleges see the value of pooling their resources with two-year institutions.

The pooling of resources in NTC/JCC has already benefited both UNT and the member community colleges in a variety of ways. UNT funds have been used to conduct the workshop Building Communities of Community Colleges and to provide ongoing administrative leadership for this consortium. Consortium funds, raised from an annual membership fee charged to each of the nine, two-year college member districts, have provided support for a major workshop on classroom research that benefited the 121 consortium faculty in attendance and UNT. Thirty of these workshop faculty indicated an interest in enrolling in the graduate school at UNT so that they could receive graduate credit for their future classroom learning and assessment projects. Other benefits to the university and member community colleges include (1) the preparation of a major grant proposal, (2) increased communication between the chancellor of UNT and the presidents or chancellors of the nine consortium colleges, and (3) the exploration of new ways to improve the transfer rates of students between consortium member colleges and UNT.

NTC/JCC provides another example of how two-year colleges and universities can work together as equal partners in the educational process. There is a realization in this partnership that both types of institutions need each other if they are to more effectively serve students in this region of the country.

Conclusion

As the challenges of the 1990s are confronted by all of higher education, the community colleges will continue to play an important role in educating the nation's work force. The community college will educate a greater number of minorities and women. More underprepared students will be entering community colleges, and there will be a greater need for develop-

mental courses. There is already increased emphasis on assessment, placement, counseling, and retention programs, and institutions are also now
focusing on standards and accountability. As educational costs rise and the
programs that community colleges administer become more costly, cooperation among community colleges is an effective way to continue to meet
the demands of the 1990s. Through collective power sharing and collective
potential, community colleges will continue to play an important role in
the educational community.

The American Association of Community and Junior Colleges (1988)
reminds institutions of the importance of building communities throughout
the academic world. The strength, the stature, and the potential of our
institutions lie in working together. The cooperative opportunities available
through consortia will help to build a strong community of institutions. As
Tollefson (1981, p. 127) says, "The consortium is a special kind of community where participation and self-direction facilitate achievement in ways
that only mature communities can enjoy." With this maturity, community
colleges will achieve increased stature, not only in the educational community but also in the civic community as a whole, as these two-year institutions play an integral part in the preparation of the work force through the
remainder of this decade and beyond.

References

American Association of Community and Junior Colleges. *Building Communities: A Vision for
a New Century.* A Report of the Commission on the Future of Community Colleges.
Washington, D.C.: American Association of Community and Junior Colleges, 1988. 58 pp.
(ED 293 578)

Fryer, T. W., Jr. "Some Tough Questions About Community Colleges." *Community, Technical,
and Junior College Journal,* 1986, 56 (6), 18-21.

Neal, D. C. "Introduction: New Roles for Consortia." In D. C. Neal (ed.), *Consortia and Interinstitutional Cooperation.* New York: Macmillan, 1988.

O'Banion, T. "Celebrating Two Decades of Innovation." *Community, Technical, and Junior
College Journal,* 1988, 58 (4), 44-46.

Patterson, L. D., and Ackley, H. C. "Introduction." In L. D. Patterson and H. C. Ackley (eds.),
*Benefits of Collegiate Cooperation: A Digest of the Costs and Benefits of Interinstitutional
Programs with Consortium Case Studies and Guidelines.* University, Ala.: Council for Interin-
stitutional Leadership, 1979. 36 pp. (ED 180 340)

Strange, D. T. "The Challenge of New Technology." In D. C. Neal (ed.), *Consortia and Interinstitutional Cooperation.* New York: Macmillan, 1988.

Tollefson, D. E. "P2E IB F4Z—Identifiers for Twenty-First Century Learning Communities."
In T. M. Stauffer (ed.), *Competition and Cooperation in American Higher Education.* Washington, D.C.: American Council on Education, 1981.

GWEN MAY is a faculty member in the computer information systems department at Richland College of the Dallas County Community College District and a doctoral student in the department of higher and adult education at the University of North Texas, Denton.

AL SMITH is professor and coordinator of higher education at Texas Technical University, Lubbock, and former director of the North Texas Community/Junior College Consortium.

Rather than waste time attempting to impress universities, community colleges should focus their efforts on building stature by striving for excellence.

To Acquire Stature: "To Thine Own Self Be True"

James O. Hammons

The time has come for community colleges to recognize what some of them already know: The only constituency with whom they need to acquire stature is themselves. For too long, community colleges have been looking to their baccalaureate-granting "big brothers" for approval, rather than following the example set by some community colleges and relying on their peers for recognition of excellence. In this chapter, I focus on those community colleges that are striving for excellence within the world of the community college.

To begin, I explain why it is virtually impossible for community colleges to acquire stature based on what nearby four-year colleges and universities think of them. Then, I describe the characteristics that contribute to excellence in a community college—in essence, the qualities that together characterize an ideal community college. I conclude by explaining why now is the time for community colleges to focus on achieving excellence.

Although this chapter is rooted in a great deal of personal experience (over five hundred separate visits to the campuses of over 170 community colleges in forty-two states and provinces), I want to acknowledge in advance that it is an opinion piece. Naturally, in those instances in which I refer to the works of others, I give them credit. But make no mistake about it, this work is the expression of one person's observations and experience—largely compiled in hotel rooms where I reflected on what I had seen, heard, or felt during visits to community college campuses.

NEW DIRECTIONS FOR COMMUNITY COLLEGES, no. 78, Summer 1992 © Jossey-Bass Publishers

Why Trying to Acquire Stature by Impressing Four-Year Institutions Is Counterproductive

There are at least two reasons that community colleges should not waste time and energy attempting to impress four-year institutions. The first reason is rooted in the dilemma that a community college president faces when trying to impress a four-year college or university. The dilemma is quite simple: Whom should one try to impress? Let us look at the alternatives, starting with the president of the university or college. How does a community college president go about trying to impress a university president? Does the process begin with a meeting, and, if so, where should it be held—on the university or the community college campus? Assuming that the meeting takes place at the community college, on what should the meeting focus to ensure the maximum positive impression? Facilities? Faculty qualifications? The success of community college transfer students at the senior institutions? And even if the university president is properly impressed, so what? It is naive and uninformed about the nature of universities and the priorities of most university presidents to assume that the invited guest is going to return to the university and extol the virtues of the community college. At best, the meeting will have impressed one person—one who will quickly explain the limits of his or her influence.

If the community college president is determined and not easily daunted, the same process can be carried out at the level of vice president, and again at the level of dean. Decisions will need to be made about whom to contact and what the focus of campus tours and meetings should be. If the meetings are fully successful, the vice president and the deans may well say, "You know, we had no idea that you community colleges were doing such a good job. We're really impressed! But you realize, of course, that the vice president and the deans at a university are not where the real power is. The strength of any university is in its departments, and department chairs are the ones with the power. That's where the real decisions are made." The number of individuals to be impressed at this level provides some indication of the enormity of the task, and the reason I would advise the community college president to "forget it."

The second reason that it is counterproductive to try to impress four-year institutions is related to the nature of universities (and many four-year colleges). Cohen and March (1973, p. 3) described universities as "organized anarchies [because the typical university] does not know what it is doing. Its goals are either vague or in dispute. . . . Its major participants wander in and out of the organization." Having spent over twenty-five years as a student and a professor at five four-year college and university campuses and having worked as a consultant on the campuses of fifteen to twenty four-year colleges, I think that these two authors are right on target. Given that, I question why a community college that is striving for excellence would be interested in seeking recognition from that kind of organization.

In addition, universities, by their very nature, are notoriously compartmentalized and inner-directed. Usually, it is only when their own self-interests are severely threatened that their actions reflect their acceptance of the idea that they exist in an open system, and they make an effort to be responsive to the needs of the society that funds them—or to the "feeder" colleges that send them students.

Defining Excellence

My article "Five Potholes in the Road to Community College Excellence" (Hammons, 1987) generated a few letters, several telephone calls, and two or three heated discussions in the hallways of several meetings. The article described "potholes" or deterrents to community colleges' achievement of or aspirations for excellence. I did not define excellence in that article. Here is a good place to do so: Excellence is "accomplishing one's mission, goals, and objectives in a cost-efficient manner, while maintaining a positive institutional climate for staff and students." In the following pages, I outline twelve characteristics that exemplify ways in which community colleges have succeeded in achieving excellence. While all of the characteristics are important, the first three are critical.

Excellent Colleges Are Clear About Their Purposes and Have Goals That Clearly Support Those Purposes. In *In Search of Excellence: Lessons from America's Best-Run Companies,* one of the most popular books on management ever published, Peters and Waterman (1982) discuss eight characteristics of successful American corporations, one of which is "stick to the knitting." While some scholars (for example, Carroll, 1983) have been quite critical of these two authors' methods and findings, my experience supports the relevance of that characteristic to community colleges, but with one caveat: Colleges cannot "stick to the knitting" if what they are knitting (I equate knitting with purposes) is not well known, agreed to, and used as the basis for decision making of all types, ranging from the criteria used in evaluating personnel to decisions about organization structure. Three clichés amplify this caveat: "If you do not know where you are going, any road will do." "If you do not know where you are going, how will you know how to get there?" "If you know where you are going, you'll know when you arrive."

Excellent Colleges Develop Action Plans (Including Budgets) Tied to Their Purposes, Goals, and Short-Term Objectives. Excellent colleges do not develop master plans that sit on shelves gathering dust. They develop the plans and then they set out to implement them. One sure indicator of the seriousness of any planning effort is the extent to which budgets and plans are related. In most colleges, planning and budgeting are like parallel lines—no matter how far they extend, they never meet. It is difficult to understand why, in an institution managed largely by persons holding doctoral degrees in educational administration, this situation exists.

In the exception-to-the-rule colleges, planning and the setting of goals and objectives are prerequisites to budgeting. In these institutions, it is a well-known and accepted way of life that expenditures for new projects or new positions can be considered only if they were earlier approved as part of the objectives for that year.

Excellent Colleges Hold Themselves Accountable. As Crosby (1979) has observed, quality is conformance to requirements. The previous characteristics are meaningless without some method of enforcing accountability.

The history of higher education clearly demonstrates that colleges and universities have consistently been criticized for lack of responsibility. But when the current accountability movement began, it did so because institutions were not *holding themselves* accountable. Many years ago, I described a four-step process by which a college could derive accountability statements (outcomes assessments) to accompany statements of mission, goals, and means for achieving them (Hammons, 1977). I concluded by observing that "the utilization of the process . . . can be a first step towards restoring public confidence in higher education" (p. 135). If community colleges had moved to implement some version of that model, they would not be drowning in the pool of accountability laws and regulations that now surround them, and the current pressure for outcomes assessment would not be required.

Excellent Colleges Have an Institutionally Approved Statement of Values. A number of colleges meet the first three criteria. It is clear where they are going, how they are going to get there, and how they will determine if they have arrived. What is missing is an understanding of how they will behave en route; in particular, how they will treat the people who make their journey possible. To date, perhaps a handful of colleges have taken the time to think through their values and put them in writing. The importance of values in business and industry is well documented in Ouchi (1981). Although written for American business, there is much about Ouchi's book that makes it worthwhile reading for community college educators. Especially helpful are the value statements in the appendices of the book.

For example, Hewlett-Packard's statement of corporate objectives says that "we are proud of the people we have in our organization, their performance and their attitude toward their jobs and toward the company. The company has been built around the individual, the personal dignity of each, and the recognition of achievements. . . . We want people to enjoy their work at H-P and to be proud of their accomplishments. This means that we must make sure that each person receives the recognition he or she needs and deserves. In the final analysis, people at all levels determine the character and strength of our company" (Ouchi, 1981, pp. 230-231). Equally of interest is Intel's statement about informal culture: "Open [constructive] confrontation is encouraged at all levels of the corporation, and is viewed as a method of problem solving and conflict resolution. Hiding problems is not acceptable. Covert political activity is strongly discouraged. Decision by consensus is the rule. Decisions once made are supported. Position in the organization is not the basis for the quality of ideas. Decisions are encouraged to be made at the lowest possible level in the organization" (Ouchi, 1981, pp. 251-252). These two statements articulate clear, succinct values that are the vital missing link in the planning documents of most colleges, even those that are well down the road to excellence.

Excellent Colleges Have an Institutionalized Human Resources Development Program. In the last twenty-five years, there have been a number of short-term, largely unsuccessful efforts at implementing staff development programs in community colleges. Today, a very optimistic estimate would be that only a small percentage of community colleges have a comprehensive human resources development program that is institutionalized, that is, an integral part of the college. To be comprehensive, the program must encompass all aspects of human resources development, including advertising, recruitment, selection, orientation, development, and evaluation. To be institutionalized, the program must be made a part of the regular budget process, not dependent on grant money or funds leftover from the budget process.

As of this writing, a doctoral student at the University of Arkansas is analyzing results from the first comprehensive, national assessment of the human resources development function in community colleges. From a preliminary review of the data, it is clear that most community colleges do not have either an institutionalized program or a comprehensive program. This finding seems somewhat incongruous given that community colleges are in the human resources development business. It places them in a situation much like that of the house painter whose house needs painting!

Excellent Colleges Have Effective Performance Appraisal Plans for All Personnel. One of the single most important ingredients in the success of any organization is a system for recognizing, rewarding, and reinforcing the performance of its people. Based on the very large number of colleges that send representatives to workshops and conferences on the topic of faculty evaluation, as well as on my own experiences in working with over fifty colleges as they attempted to develop a way of evaluating faculty and managerial performance, it is clear that evaluation is a problem with which most community colleges are still wrestling. In this regard, one observation must be made: Whether performance plans are used for developmental or judgmental purposes does not appear to be as important as whether employees know what their supervisors think about their performance and whether employees believe that their productive performance is being recognized, rewarded, and reinforced.

Excellent Colleges Adapt to Environmental-Social Changes. Compared to the ages of many four-year colleges, most of today's community colleges are in their infancy. In fact, for many, most of their "charter" faculty are still active. Yet, a surprising number of these institutions are just as steeped in tradition or as set in their ways as some of the oldest of the four-year colleges.

The history of the community college is a history of change. Some analysts of the community college are convinced that this ability to adapt to change has been a major factor behind the success of the community college. The excellent colleges are the ones whose environmental antennae are out and working, whose internal climate sensors are on and registering, and whose administrations are not afraid to rethink priorities, to change direction, and to add or drop programs when social climate and environmental factors indicate that it is appropriate to do so.

Excellent Colleges Manage Their Resources Wisely. More than twenty years ago, there appeared marked differences in the ways that colleges with essentially the same funding sources managed their resources. It was often all I could do to keep a straight face while a president or dean explained that he (and in those days, almost all were male) would like to do something or make some change but "there just wasn't any money for that," when I had been on the campus of another college in the same state that was doing precisely what he said could not be done. Since then, the differences in how colleges use resources no longer surprise me—only the degree to which a lack of funding is used as an excuse or barrier to making needed changes.

A detailed discussion of the ways that community colleges might be more efficient is a topic worthy of a treatise. For now, the four areas where differences in efficient use of resources are most obvious warrant mention. These four areas are administrative structure, new-course controls, course scheduling, and use of technology.

In the area of administrative structure, some institutions seem to have administrators who multiply like amoebas. For every new vice presidency created, there will soon appear an associate vice president, who will soon acquire his or her own administrative assistant or executive secretary. The effects of this practice are devastating—to faculty morale, to communication, and to budget. All too often, these top-heavy institutions have secretarial pools with 1:20 ratios for faculty and administrators who complain of not having enough money for staff development.

The number of courses offered and the manner in which they are scheduled are two other areas where particularly inefficient management practices are often found. At one time, the typical community college curriculum could be likened to a stripped-down Chevrolet—it got us where we wanted to go, but with very few "extras." Not anymore. Today, it is common to find a Cadillac-style list of course offerings that equals or even exceeds the bloated offerings of nearby four-year colleges. Over two decades ago, Dressel (1971) illustrated how, in the absence of significant infusions of new money, course proliferation results in lower salary increases, increased scheduling problems, and classroom shortages. The accuracy of his predictions is quite evident today.

Colleges also waste dollars in determining the number of multisection courses to be scheduled. At institutions such as Miami-Dade Community College, the average size of classes within a division is a carefully determined goal that division chairs must achieve. Because of the resultant savings in their academic budget, significant dollars are available for other activities, such as faculty travel. Again, it is safe to say that colleges that are not careful in controlling class scheduling are often the same ones that complain about "not having any money."

Another resource that is used differently by the excellence-oriented colleges is minutes—the time of their people. The differences between the two types of colleges can be understood only after recognizing that community colleges are labor-intensive organizations in which personnel costs often consume over three-fourths of the budgets, and in which, with few exceptions, most personnel are paid by the hour.

In the non-excellence-oriented colleges, staff, faculty, and upper-level administrators often pay little regard to the person-hours that tasks require. Inefficient methods and redundant operations constitute standard operating procedure. The routine is *not* routinized ("Let's see, how will we handle registration this time?"), and staff and faculty are often required to continue using outmoded time wasters such as ditto machines and manual typewriters.

In contrast, excellence-oriented colleges view their people as their most valuable and costly resource. They recognize the value of "routinizing the routine" (without "rut-inizing"), and they look for ways to make the job of each person as meaningful and financially rewarding as possible. As a consequence, they are quite receptive to the use of technology, both to increase efficiency and to ensure that their people are not required to do what machines can do better.

Excellent Colleges Seek to Identify and Solve Their Problems. Lewin (1947) suggested that excellent institutions are institutions that can solve their own problems. The truth in this observation is obvious. But before a college can solve a problem, it has to recognize and accept that the problem exists. Over the years, the colleges that have impressed me have been those that seem to actually enjoy finding problems. A problem identified was an opportunity to learn how to improve, and they welcomed it! Further, once a problem was identified, the search for a solution brought out the best in their people.

In the other-than-ideal colleges, a very different attitude toward problems exists. Mostly, problems are dreaded, and there is often a reluctance to admit that a problem exists, which is sometimes tied to the mistaken notion that the presence of a problem is prima facia evidence of wrongdoing. In other instances, once it is recognized that a problem exists, there is usually a long delay (often filled by attempts at blame placing) before the organization finds and implements an effective method of resolving it.

Excellent Colleges Have an Effective Way of Involving Their Various Constituencies in College Governance. The board of trustees is the legal governing body of most community colleges, and in less-than-excellent colleges that point is repeatedly emphasized as a reason why something cannot be done: "They [the board] would have to approve that" or "It's board policy." In the college oriented toward excellence, the board is recognized for what it is—a legally constituted body with specific responsibilities and accountabilities. The board, the president and his or her staff, the deans and vice presidents and their staffs, the faculty senate, the student council, the staff society, and the faculty association are all seen as individuals or groups who have a vested interest in the welfare of their constituents *and* who have the interests of the college as a whole to consider. In these institutions, great effort is made to delineate the authority, responsibility, and accountability of each group so that conflict is minimized, and at all times they strive to observe the primary underlying principle of any effective shared governance system: Those affected by a decision must be involved in the decision making.

Excellent Colleges Believe in Teamwork and Practice a Team Approach. In the ideal college, there is a conscious decision to work as a team, and individual members are willing to put aside self-interests for the good of the team. This decision often has a synergistic effect, where group output is better than might have been expected given the talents of individual members. In this kind of work environment, team members look forward to coming to work and even enjoy spending time with other team members and their families away from work.

A lack of teamwork usually characterizes less than ideal colleges, where enlightened self-interest prevails and an "everyone for themselves" mentality exists. The result is often one or two "stars" who succeed in pursuing their own agendas (then use that achievement to move on to other institutions while leaving behind messes for someone else to clean up), a "we-they" mentality that can result in duplication or missed opportunity, and a work climate best characterized as somewhere between totally unbearable and just barely tolerable.

Excellent Colleges Have Effective Communication Systems. Effective communication is the glue that holds a college together. Without effective communication, attempts to do the things that lead to excellence—plan and set goals, recognize and solve problems, and function as a team—are all doomed to fail. As a consequence, in the excellence-oriented college, all parties—board, administration, faculty, and classified staff—recognize that good communication is something that takes effort, and everyone works as hard at listening to one another as they do at ensuring that they are sending clear messages. In these institutions, most people usually think that they know what is going on, and when they do not know, they are not afraid to speak up and do not hesitate to "go to the horse's mouth" to get the true story.

In contrast, in institutions with poor communication, rumors are rampant. In these colleges, people expend a great deal of energy to find out what is going on, the prevailing mode of communication is one-way via written messages, and people rarely speak their minds. As a consequence, any attempt to make significant improvements is doomed to fail.

One additional observation must be made. The size of the institution or the presence or absence of detailed governance mechanisms appears to have little relationship to effective communication. There are small colleges with fewer than fifty faculty that have major communication problems, and there are large colleges that, on paper, have little in the way of shared governance structures in place but have staffs who are well-informed about what is going on and believe that they have an appropriate role in decision making.

Conclusion: The Importance of Now

It is especially critical at this time in their history for community colleges to focus on improving their performance and on impressing themselves and their communities with their worth. First, there is the importance of now. Virtually any well-informed individual is aware that our country is at a crossroads in the international economic community. Our choices are simple. We can elect to change course and move in the direction of a higher quality of life, or we can continue on our present route, which has led us to drop several notches below our former position of number one in the world. The choice is ours. The task of improving the quality of the education of our youth, our work force, and our citizens must be our first priority. Once that goal is achieved, the benefits that will follow include a well-informed electorate, a renewed interest in participating in local, state, and federal elections, an environmentally conscious citizenry, a "kinder, gentler society," and a higher quality of living for all of us—in short, the kind of society that we once thought possible.

Obviously, community college leaders alone cannot effect these changes, but they can get their own houses in order! In all likelihood, community colleges will continue to be the only chance for postsecondary education for hundreds of thousands of high school graduates. Community colleges are already the only hope for millions of persons who are beyond high school age and who are living and working in our communities, many in jobs that will not exist five years from now.

The challenges facing community colleges are too urgent for them to waste valuable time trying to impress and change the attitudes of university types. Instead, their energies should be directed at getting on with their major task—that of achieving excellence. By focusing on this goal, community colleges will be doing what is right for the only groups that they should be trying to impress: their communities, their students, and their own staffs! In this regard, the only mission that a community college has is to provide the highest quality, postsecondary educational services possible to the citizens of its community. This is a very simple, straightforward mission. It is a mission around which staff can rally because, even in today's materialistic society, it is a mission that is worthy of the devotion of those who staff the "people's college"—if they perceive that their institution is seriously interested in pursuing it.

References

Carroll, D. T. "A Disappointing Search for Excellence." *Harvard Business Review*, 1983, *61* (6), 78–88.

Cohen, M. D., and March, J. G. *Leadership and Ambiguity: The American College President*. Highstown, N.J.: McGraw-Hill, 1974.

Crosby, P. B. *Quality Is Free: The Art of Making Quality Certain*. New York: McGraw-Hill, 1979.

Dressel, P. L. *College and University Curriculum*. Berkeley, Calif.: McCutchan, 1971.

Hammons, J. O. "Establishing a Charter of Accountability: A Process for Operationalizing Institutional Goals and Objectives." *Journal of Thought*, 1977, *12* (2), 129–135.

Hammons, J. O. "Five Potholes in the Road to Community College Excellence." *Community College Review*, 1987, *15* (1), 5–12.

Lewin, K. *The Research Center for Group Dynamics*. New York: Beacon House, 1947.

Ouchi, W. *Theory Z: How American Business Can Meet the Japanese Challenge*. Reading, Mass.: Addison-Wesley, 1981.

Peters, T. J., and Waterman, R. H., Jr. *In Search of Excellence: Lessons from America's Best-Run Companies*. New York: Harper & Row, 1982.

JAMES O. HAMMONS is professor and coordinator of the graduate program in higher education leadership at the University of Arkansas, Fayetteville, and has served as consultant to more than 170 community colleges in forty-two states and provinces.

This chapter presents current literature on the relationship
between community colleges and baccalaureate institutions, as
well as on issues regarding the quality of two-year colleges.

Sources and Information: Community Colleges and Issues of Articulation and Quality

Diane Hirshberg

This volume focuses on a number of issues regarding the relationship between community colleges and baccalaureate institutions. In addition to direct collaboration between these institutions, for purposes such as facilitating transfer or improving minority student achievement in higher education, the volume addresses the question of the quality of education in two-year colleges, and the importance of striving for excellence.

There are a number of examples of productive relationships between two- and four-year institutions designed to improve minority student achievement, facilitate transfer between institutions, and strengthen the teaching and research functions of schools at both levels. This chapter provides an overview of some of the current literature in the ERIC data base on these topics. Most ERIC documents (references with "ED" numbers) can be read on microfiche at over eight hundred libraries worldwide. In addition, most can be ordered on microfiche or paper copy from the ERIC Document Reproduction Service at (800) 443-ERIC. Journal articles are not available from this agency. Most journal articles can be acquired through regular library channels or purchased for $10.75 per copy from UMI Articles Clearinghouse at (800) 521-0600, extension 533.

Facilitating Transfer Between Community Colleges and Baccalaureate Institutions

In several states, community college and university systems have developed articulation agreements that set forth course requirements and curricula to facilitate transfer from community colleges to four-year institutions. Banks and Byock (1991) describe the Transfer Alliance Program (TAP) at the University of California at Los Angeles (UCLA), which involves curriculum articulation efforts between UCLA and twelve Los Angeles County community colleges. UCLA and the participating colleges maintain a set of mutually determined commitments that require the colleges to establish a formal program structure, offer a core of enriched courses, encourage underrepresented minority student participation, and promote relationships with high schools and between university and community college faculty. The TAP curriculum consists of a core of enriched general education courses in which students engage in extensive writing, reading, and research. An evaluation of the program found quite positive results. TAP faculty showed more concern for the transfer process, engaged in greater experimentation with teaching methods, and developed more student-focused classrooms than did non-TAP faculty. TAP students demonstrated better class attendance, preparation, and understanding of ideas than did non-TAP students; TAP students and faculty interacted more than their non-TAP counterparts. Statewide, TAP colleges had higher percentages of students transferring to the University of California than achieved by non-TAP colleges; and TAP transfer students had higher grade point averages and persistence rates than non-TAP transfer students at UCLA.

In 1988, California State Assembly Bill 1725 directed the governing boards of the University of California (UC), the California State University (CSU), and the California Community Colleges to jointly develop, maintain, disseminate, and adopt a common core curriculum in general education for the purpose of facilitating student transfer between all state institutions. As Cepeda (1991) explains, in 1986 all three academic senates had already begun work on a common curriculum in response to recommendations from the California legislature's Review of the Master Plan for Higher Education. By February 1990, all three senates had approved the curriculum, with implementation scheduled for fall 1991. The result was the Intersegmental General Education Transfer Curriculum, completion of which permits a student to transfer from a community college to the CSU or UC system without taking additional general education courses to satisfy campus general education requirements. Courses in this curriculum include the following subject areas: English/communications, mathematics, arts and humanities, social and behavioral sciences, and foreign languages.

Also in California, San Joaquin Delta College and CSU-Stanislaus have jointly developed programs that lead to seven baccalaureate and two master's degrees. Students can combine courses from the college and from the CSU Stockton Center to earn degrees without having to leave their area. This program represents an outgrowth of a commitment from both community colleges and the state university system to provide quality education at a reasonable cost (Ostar, 1991).

In Florida, an articulation agreement guaranteeing the transferability of a set of community college general education courses to the state's universities has been in place since 1959. Harden (1991) describes this agreement and its evolution over the years. A new agreement, accepted by Florida's community colleges and universities in 1971, defined the Associate in Arts (A.A.) degree as a two-year transfer degree and established an Articulation Coordination Committee, common course numbering, and a common academic calendar. Subsequent amendments guaranteed A.A. degree students admission to the state university system as well as the transferability of any course in the system. In order to achieve a common calendar, all twenty-eight community colleges and nine state universities elected to operate on the semester system. Other statewide efforts to improve articulation include the following: (1) All of the universities and a number of the two-year colleges employ designated articulation officers who coordinate articulation efforts and resolve difficulties in the articulation process. (2) University articulation officers participate in annual visits to community colleges to meet with faculty, administrators, and prospective transfer students. (3) Each of the universities publishes articulation manuals for community college counselors to help in advising students on admissions and transfer policies. (4) Computerized advisement programs help students develop course plans and determine course requirements. And (5) orientation programs and special scholarships are in place to assist transfer students.

Improving Outcomes for Minority Students

Concern about increasing the number of minority students entering and completing degrees at four-year institutions has led to a number of innovative cooperative programs between community colleges and universities. Grossbach (1991) describes a joint effort between the Community College of Philadelphia (CCP) and LaSalle and Temple universities in Philadelphia to improve student transfer between the institutions, focusing especially on the enrollment and transfer of minority students. CCP coordinated an initial one-week workshop in 1989, assembling a total of thirty faculty representatives from the three schools. Workshop organizers argued that if faculty across colleges developed a sense of common classroom practices, this would eventually percolate up to the administrative levels where articulation agreements are hammered out. As an outgrowth of the workshop, six working groups were formed in fall 1989, representing the disciplines of physical sciences, history, mathematics, English, social sciences, and foreign languages. Faculty members from the three colleges participated in five two-hour meetings held for each discipline. These discussions covered issues pertaining to course syllabi, exams and writing assignments, appropriate reading materials, sequencing of courses, and criteria for mathematics literacy. These meetings served as preparation for a two-day conference planned for the following spring, which brought together 150 educators from two- and four-year institutions across Pennsylvania. The workshops and discussion groups, shaped by the members of the original six disciplinary committees, focused on course content and classroom teaching.

Lieberman (1991) describes the Exploring Transfer Program, created by LaGuardia Community College and Vassar College in New York to improve the achievement of poor and minority students in higher education. The two schools have developed a successful residential summer learning experience to raise educational aspirations of poor and minority students and attract students to four-year colleges. Students are team-taught by faculty from both institutions, live in a Vassar dormitory with a member of the Vassar faculty, and receive instruction in the use of Vassar's academic resources. Now in its seventh year, the program has had dramatic success; more than 70 percent of the students who have participated in the Exploring Transfer Program have transferred to four-year institutions, and the Ford Foundation is now funding a replication program for five other collaborations between two- and four-year institutions.

In New York, innovative programs are being designed to increase the number of minority students both achieving baccalaureate degrees and entering the teaching profession. These programs utilize the resources of both community colleges and state four-year schools. They allow minority students to enter teacher education programs at two-year institutions, transfer to four-year teacher preparation institutions without loss of academic credit, and be eligible for initial state teacher certification upon graduation (New York State Education Department, 1990).

Partnerships to Strengthen Institutions

Not all partnerships between two- and four-year institutions are designed solely to promote student transfer and achievement; some are intended instead to strengthen the quality of the institutions involved. Wallenfeldt and Anglin (1990) describe the partnership for educational progress between Cuyahoga Community College (CCC) and Kent State University (KSU), which has evolved over nearly two decades of continuous communication and political obstacles. The foundation for the partnership was established in the early 1970s, a time rife with community college criticism of the inadequacy of higher education programs for training two-year college personnel and with university criticism of the open-door policies of two-year colleges. While efforts in the 1970s to develop a doctoral program at KSU to address the skills required of community college educators failed, a community college specialist was added to the KSU faculty in 1979, and informal relations between the institutions continued. Aided and supported by interested KSU and CCC faculty and administrators, twelve CCC faculty members enrolled in doctoral programs at KSU. The High Schools for the Future Project, developed and jointly administered by KSU and CCC senior faculty, led to a joint staff development program for CCC faculty, which was approved in 1987. The success of these and additional collaborative efforts has created a solid working partnership between the two institutions.

Improving Quality

There are many factors that contribute to excellence in the community college. The quality of instruction is the factor that most people would recognize; however, Vaughan (this volume) argues that faculty scholarship is also an important component for achieving excellence. Knowledge about what constitutes excellence in a community college is necessary to achieving it, as is the ability to measure excellence via student outcomes or other indicators.

Cassel (1990) presents the definitions and indicators of "quality" higher education provided by twenty presidents of two- and four-year colleges. She found seven different definitions of quality in use among these administrators: "(1) accomplishment of the institutional mission, (2) results of the investment of resources to develop the competencies and skills of those whom [they] serve, (3) the amount and type of responsiveness to student needs, (4) positive expectations for the college and students, (5) the contribution the institution makes to the welfare of its community, (6) how well the institution functions to maximize its resources, (7) attention to the details of the academic programs and campus environment that impact faculty and students" (1990, p. 289). The indicators of quality that these presidents use include employment or continuing education success of graduates; student outcomes such as grade point average and exit exams; management issues such as achievement of mission, adequacy of resources, and utilization of certain management techniques; quality of faculty and learning environment measures such as class size, faculty credentials, and staff development practices; and student opinions regarding the institutions.

Community colleges indeed may not be challenging their students to the same degree that four-year institutions do. Taylor and Rendón (1991) conducted a comparison of the academic rigor and cultural diversity of U.S. history curricula in North Carolina's community colleges and universities. They focused on whether survey courses and assignments were comparable at two- and four-year institutions, and whether women's and minorities' perspectives and local history were included in survey courses and electives. Taylor and Rendón found that some of the community college courses in American history were less rigorous than those offered in four-year institutions. They concluded that examinations, reading, and writing assignments all needed to be strengthened in the colleges. In addition, they believe that while community college faculty are successful in incorporating multicultural perspectives into survey courses, the use of assignments focusing on minorities needs to be increased.

In order to improve the quality of education at community colleges, several actions can be taken. Hiring of quality faculty is an obvious action. Coady (1990) describes how Edison State Community College in Ohio uses the techniques of descriptive interviewing and teaching simulations to select new faculty and avoid the costs to the college and its students of making poor hiring decisions. In descriptive interviewing, questions focus on how the candidate has actually behaved in real situations rather than on vague philosophical issues and hypothetical solutions to hypothetical problems. For example, during traditional interviews, candidates might be asked to describe a good evaluation system. In a descriptive interview the candidate would be asked to describe the evaluation system that he or she actually used in the most recent course taught, whether it was normative or criterion-based, and what kinds of tests and exercises were used. Other sequences of questions used at Edison focus on the candidates' past experience with curriculum development and professional activities to maintain discipline currency. Given that even the most informative and revealing interview does not necessarily guarantee a good teacher, the college also uses teaching simulations to assess how well a candidate relates to students and how coherently he or she can deliver information and stimulate thinking. Finalists are asked to choose their own mode of delivery and to cover a small body of material in real or mock classes. The evaluation system for the simulation consists of solicited feedback about the candidate's presentation from the students and any nonfaculty before the department representative, the division chair, and the search committee meet for discussion. Although pitfalls exist in both methods, the combination offers a more solid base for hiring decisions than does the traditional interview and résumé.

The characteristics of an excellent teacher are the subject of a study by Baker, Roueche, and Gillett-Karam (1990). Drawing from interviews with 869 award-winning community college professors and instructors from the United States and Canada, the researchers describe the behaviors and techniques used by outstanding teachers in their roles as leaders, influencers, and motivators. The researchers provide a foundation for the concept of teacher as leader, including operational definitions of "teaching" and "learning" and a discussion of motivation theories. They demonstrate the clear link between leaders and followers, highlighting the path-goal model of leadership as a process of gathering behavioral information about teaching. In addition, they present ways to predict the behavior of effective teachers, develop recommendations for improvement through self-evaluation, and explain ways in which effective teachers motivate students.

As Cassel (1990) pointed out, in addition to excellence in teaching, other factors contribute to quality at the community college. Identification and measurement of these factors can be a difficult task; however, some colleges have developed models for addressing this challenge. St. Petersburg Junior College (SPJC) developed a program to include the entire campus in determining and planning for excellence within the college. In 1989, the Focus on Access, Community, and Excellence in Teaching (FACET) Commission was created at SPJC to develop recommendations to guide the college into the twenty-first century (FACET Commission, 1990). The commission's work plan included the definition of SPJC's educational standards; open hearings to solicit ideas from students, faculty, alumni, administration, staff, and community; and the exploration of ways to enrich teaching effectiveness. The investigation of the college's institutional values concluded that, above all, SPJC exists to serve students and to provide educational opportunities for its multicultural community. The guiding principles developed for the college underscored the value of people, academic excellence, partnerships, innovation and creativity, and leadership. The commission's findings with respect to employee selection, orientation, and evaluation; pay and professional recognition; faculty and staff development; and organization and program development resulted in a series of recommendations for improvement. Selected recommendations stress that (1) selection processes ensure that candidates understand and support SPJC's mission, (2) orientation procedures be expanded, (3) evaluation focus on both appraising and improving performance, (4) a faculty ranking system be established based on performance, longevity, credentials, and service, (5) outstanding achievement be recognized and rewarded, (6) a long-range plan for faculty and staff development be developed, and (7) SPJC continue to focus on student success and minority achievement and implement new efforts in the areas of applied ethics and work force literacy.

Herder, Edmunds, Gwynn, and Hanieski (1990) present a rationale and model for measuring instructional quality, drawing from the experiences of Lansing Community College (LCC). The tools used to measure instructional quality at LCC include external accreditation, student and graduate surveys, and standardized student evaluation of instruction. The criteria used to review departments and programs include clear and results-oriented purpose and mission, course organization and management, external testing results, basic skills of entering students, and class visitation results. LCC uses incentives and rewards for promoting excellence and creativity, including annual distinguished faculty, administrator, and staff awards, and awards for honors students and other high-achieving students. There is strong evidence that LCC is effectively fulfilling its role, including the fact that the college has a clear, shared, and achievable mission and that a logical, data-based system is used to verify progress toward excellence.

Community colleges recently have had an opportunity to participate in a pilot project to improve their educational quality. Cowart (1990) describes the development and activities of Project Cooperation, a demonstration project to help institutions improve educational effectiveness by employing outcomes measures and assessment strategies. The project includes several activities, including a national survey, research on different plans and models at demonstration sites, summer workshops, and institutional effectiveness workshops. Institutions can serve as project demonstration sites by developing and implementing model student assessment practices using American College Testing Program instruments. To participate, colleges must decide on the "value-added" or "predictive" assessment effort to be undertaken, identify the factors critical to project success and ways to achieve success, and successfully implement the plan. Cowart outlines the stages in developing the project proposal and implementation plan, along with the purposes of each stage.

Hudgins (1991), too, believes that institutional assessment is a valuable tool for achieving excellence in community colleges. He argues that efforts to assess institutional effectiveness not only enable community colleges to meet accreditation mandates but also can serve as a catalyst for institutional renewal. Institutional effectiveness has become an important topic for the 1990s as a result of past neglect of accountability, new legislative mandates for education, changes in accreditation criteria from process-oriented to outcomes-oriented, and renewed interest by colleges in improving the quality of their instruction. To assess institutional effectiveness, a college must define its mission, articulate the major results that are expected from the achievement of that mission, and define the specific evidence that will be acceptable to determine whether those results have been achieved. At a minimum, institutional assessment processes require the institution to (1) articulate its mission, (2) establish a planning mechanism, (3) develop an evaluation system, (4) identify critical areas of success, (5) establish priority standards on which to judge effectiveness, (6) determine mechanisms for documenting whether the established standards have been met, and (7) utilize the results of assessment for decision making. In addition, the institution must enlist the support of the president and board of trustees, involve all institutional units, and determine how to pay for assessment. Indicators of effectiveness might include transfer student success, job placement rates of graduates, employer satisfaction, and economic impact of the institution. Institutions should publicly recognize individuals and departments that make significant contributions toward achievement of their missions.

Faculty engagement in scholarship activities is an important component of the effort to achieve excellence in community colleges. Vaughan (1991, p. 5) argues that community college faculty and administrators must adopt a new view of scholarship, broadening the definition in a way "that conforms to and enhances fulfillment of the community college mission." He argues that book reviews, annotated bibliographies, lectures, non-research-based articles in journals, and so forth constitute scholarship, as much as do traditional research projects. Bell (1990) found that in Ontario, Canada, community college instructors were engaging in scholarship activities that meet this broadened definition. He looked at the research activities of faculty at seven community colleges in Ontario. Faculty were asked to indicate how often they participated in twenty-two different research activities and how characteristic these activities were of their role as community college faculty. Bell's primary interest in the study was to determine whether community college faculty were using the traditional university definition of what constitutes research (publishing) as a basis for defining their research role, as compared to a broader definition of what constitutes research in the community college environment (applied expertise). Results showed that a small core of community college faculty were engaged in traditional university research activities such as reviewing proposals for funding agencies, publishing or editing books and monographs, and delivering papers to professional society meetings. But, on the whole, community college faculty were more likely to engage in research activities related to the applied mission of the community college. These data suggest that future research should examine what these results mean in terms of teaching effectiveness, institutional quality, and overall faculty job satisfaction and productivity.

Community colleges can serve a specialized role in the field of education research. Cross (1990) argues that the mission, curricula, students, and faculty of community colleges make them ideal laboratories for the study of teaching and learning at the college level. To accomplish this goal, community college faculty members should take on the role of classroom researchers, conducting careful, systematic, and patient studies of their students engaged in the learning process. The purpose of classroom research is to help teachers assess the effectiveness of their own teaching, so that they can make appropriate modifications while their classes are still in progress. One form of classroom assessment solicits feedback on how students are learning. At the end of each class period, students are asked to write down the most important thing learned that day and to identify any remaining questions. Community colleges are in the best position to be leaders in developing expertise in college-level teaching for the following reasons: (1) Community colleges are primarily teaching institutions. (2) No other type of institution has the same challenge or obligation for teaching excellence. (3) The diverse community college curriculum offers a potentially productive laboratory for gaining knowledge about learning. (4) Classroom teaching is especially important to commuter students, who constitute virtually all of the community college student population. (5) The practical orientation of community college teachers ensures that the problems for classroom research are real and that they affect college teachers in their classrooms. And (6) the diversity of the community college student population is an advantage in studying the learning process.

Community colleges fulfill a unique role in higher education. They provide opportunities to students who otherwise might be excluded from postsecondary study, and they offer services to the community that are often unavailable elsewhere. As the documents in this chapter point out, the quality of the education and services provided in the community college can be enhanced through partnerships with baccalaureate institutions as well as through self-study and improvement activities.

References

Baker, G. A., III, Roueche, J. E., and Gillett-Karam, R. *Teaching as Leading: Profiles of Excellence in the Open-Door College.* Washington, D.C.: American Association of Community and Junior Colleges, 1990.

Banks, D. L., and Byock, G. *The Effects of the Transfer Alliance Program on Its Colleges, Faculty, and Students.* Los Angeles: Office of Academic Interinstitutional Programs, University of California, Los Angeles, 1991. 210 pp. (ED 332 761)

Bell, S. "Research Activities of Community College Faculty: Experience at the Ontario Colleges of Applied Arts and Technology." Paper presented at the annual forum of the Association for Institutional Research, Louisville, Kentucky, May 1990. 26 pp. (ED 321 695)

Cassel, M. "The Elusive Concept of Quality: What Junior and Senior College Presidents Think." *Community/Junior College Quarterly of Research and Practice,* 1990, *14* (4), 285–296.

Cepeda, R. *Adoption of the Intersegmental General Education Transfer Curriculum.* Sacramento: California Community Colleges, Office of the Chancellor, 1991. 17 pp. (ED 326 271)

Coady, S. "How to Hire Good Faculty." Paper presented at the 12th annual international conference on Teaching Excellence, Austin, Texas, May 1990. 15 pp. (ED 320 644)

Cowart, S. C. *Project Cooperation: A Joint Effort of Community College Educators and ACT to Answer Questions About Institutional Effectiveness and Outcomes Assessment.* Washington, D.C.: American Association of Community and Junior Colleges, 1990. 27 pp. (ED 322 946)

Cross, K. P. "Celebrating Excellence in the Classroom." Paper presented at the 12th international conference on Teaching Excellence, Austin, Texas, May 1990. 24 pp. (ED 320 625)

Focus on Access, Community, and Excellence in Teaching (FACET) Commission. *The FACET Report. Toward 2001: An Odyssey of Excellence.* St. Petersburg, Fla.: St. Petersburg Junior College, 1990. 30 pp. (ED 319 418)

Grossbach, B. L. *Generating Faculty Dialogue Across Colleges: A Personal Experience.* Transfer Working Papers, vol. 2, no. 1. Washington, D.C.: American Council on Education, National Center for Academic Achievement and Transfer, 1991. 14 pp. (ED 327 245)

Harden, H. D. "Challenges of Articulation Between Sectors." Paper presented at Florida State University's national conference on Celebrating Leadership for the 21st Century, Tallahassee, Florida, March 1991. 13 pp. (ED 331 559)

Herder, D. M., Edmunds, P. A., Gwynn, V. N., and Hanieski, D. "Instructional Quality Assurance at Lansing Community College." Panel discussion presented at the 2nd annual summer institute conference of the Consortium for Institutional Effectiveness and Student Success, Toronto, Canada, June 1990. 90 pp. (ED 320 634)

Hudgins, J. *Institutional Effectiveness: A Strategy for Institutional Renewal.* Columbia, S.C.: Midlands Technical College, 1991. 13 pp. (ED 335 087)

Lieberman, J. E. "The La Guardia-Vassar Connection." *Educational Record,* 1991, 72 (2), 43–45.

New York State Education Department. Office of Higher and Professional Education. *Developing Jointly Registered Teacher Education Programs to Increase Minority Baccalaureate Achievement.* Proceedings of a Statewide Invitational Conference of Two- and Four-Year Colleges. Albany: New York State Education Department, 1990. 84 pp. (ED 332 991)

Ostar, A. W. "Community Colleges and State Colleges and Universities: A Natural Partnership." *Community, Technical, and Junior College Journal*, 1991, *61* (5), 21-25.

Taylor, M. T., and Rendón, L. I. "The American History Curriculum in North Carolina's Public Community Colleges and Universities: A Comparative Study." *Community College Review*, 1991, *19* (1), 36-41.

Vaughan, G. B. "Scholarship and the Community College Professional: Focusing the Debate." In G. B. Vaughan and J. C. Palmer (eds.), *Enhancing Teaching and Administration Through Scholarship*. New Directions for Community Colleges, no. 76. San Francisco: Jossey-Bass, 1991.

Wallenfeldt, E. C., and Anglin, L. W. *Institutional Partnership: An Evolving Case Study*. Kent, Ohio: Graduate School of Education, Kent State University, 1990. 16 pp. (ED 326 279)

DIANE HIRSHBERG is user services coordinator at the ERIC Clearinghouse for Junior Colleges, University of California, Los Angeles.

INDEX

ORDERING INFORMATION

NEW DIRECTIONS FOR COMMUNITY COLLEGES is a series of paperback books that provides expert assistance to help community colleges meet the challenges of their distinctive and expanding educational mission. Books in the series are published quarterly in Fall, Winter, Spring, and Summer and are available for purchase by subscription as well as by single copy.

SUBSCRIPTIONS for 1992 cost $48.00 for individuals (a savings of 20 percent over single-copy prices) and $70.00 for institutions, agencies, and libraries. Please do not send institutional checks for personal subscriptions. Standing orders are accepted.

SINGLE COPIES cost $15.95 when payment accompanies order. (California, New Jersey, New York, and Washington, D.C., residents please include appropriate sales tax.) Billed orders will be charged postage and handling.

DISCOUNTS FOR QUANTITY ORDERS are available. Please write to the address below for information.

ALL ORDERS must include either the name of an individual or an official purchase order number. Please submit your order as follows:
    Subscriptions: specify series and year subscription is to begin
    Single copies: include individual title code (such as CC1)

MAIL ALL ORDERS TO:
    Jossey-Bass Publishers
    350 Sansome Street
    San Francisco, California 94104

FOR SALES OUTSIDE OF THE UNITED STATES CONTACT:
    Maxwell Macmillan International Publishing Group
    866 Third Avenue
    New York, New York 10022

OTHER TITLES AVAILABLE IN THE
NEW DIRECTIONS FOR COMMUNITY COLLEGES SERIES
Arthur M. Cohen, Editor-in-Chief
Florence B. Brawer, Associate Editor